CHARACTERS AND EVENTS
OF
ROMAN HISTORY

CHARACTERS AND EVENTS
OF
ROMAN HISTORY

From Cæsar to Nero

Guglielmo Ferrero, Litt. D.

Introduction by Paul McKechnie

BARNES
& NOBLE
BOOKS
NEW YORK

CONTENTS

INTRODUCTION

In 1909, intellectual superstar Guglielmo Ferrero toured the northeast of the USA, accepted an honorary degree, and lectured about Roman history. *Characters and Events of Roman History* is the book of his lectures. It presents a lively selection of people and events: Julius Caesar, Antony and Cleopatra, the Emperor Nero— and a chapter about the importance of wine to the growth of Rome. The response was warm. Ferrero, who had traveled widely in the European continent, argued that "Rome is in the mental field the strongest bond that holds together the most diverse peoples of Europe." Throughout *Characters and Events of Roman History*, Ferrero explores the curious paradox of what Roman authors meant when they claimed that Rome lacked its ancient vigour and was fatally weakened by corruption—at the very moment when (as we see it today) it was for the first time reaching the full extent of its power. As he treats these questions, Ferrero also reflects on his own times, on the brink of the new (twentieth) century. Frances Lance Ferrero, the author's sister-in-law, translated the lectures into English.

Born in 1871 in a middle-class Italian family, Guglielmo Ferrero started out as a law student and student radical in Pisa, then Turin. Curiosity and left-wing idealism impelled him into the growing field of criminology. After traveling across much of Europe in the mid-1890s, Ferrero in 1897 wrote *L'Europa giovane* (*Young Europe*), a book which caused a continent-wide sensation. Offers followed, and Ferrero chose to write columns for *Il secolo*, a Milan daily paper, and used the financial security gained from this to continue as a book author. In 1902, he announced that he would write a history of Rome: Its five volumes occupied more or less the next five years of his life. In 1908, invited by President Theodore Roosevelt, he visited the United States and gave the lectures that form *Characters and Events of Roman History*. With the rise of Mussolini, Ferrero became an opposition figure in Italy. He argued that protest and open opposition were the right reaction to Fascism; but he lost his newspaper column and spent much of the later 1920s living out of the public eye. Allowed to leave Italy in 1930, Ferrero became a professor of contemporary history in the University of Geneva, a job he held until his death in 1942.

The "Ferrero phenomenon" had gripped Europe for a decade by the time President Roosevelt invited Ferrero to the White House. He exemplifies a kind of social climbing—in his case, from solid middle-class to internationally lionized hero—of which he writes in general terms in the first chapter of this book: "In the new generation," he says, "the children. . .started where the previous generation left off, and therefore wish to gain yet new enjoyments, different from and greater than those they obtained without trouble through the efforts of the preceding generation." Ferrero had a brilliant student career. He enrolled at the University of Pisa in 1888, then in the following year visited Turin with a group of fellow-students and was introduced to Cesare Lombroso, who persuaded him to continue his university education there. Later, in 1901, Ferrero married Lombroso's daughter Gina. Ferrero's undergraduate dissertation of 1891 was published as his first book, *Il simbolo* (*Symbol*), in 1893.

The left-wing ideas which impelled Ferrero to become a founder member, in 1889, of the *Associazione radicale universitaria* (University Radical Association), went on shaping his intellectual development. He seemed destined for an academic career. But an instinct for an audience beyond the academic milieu showed in the choice of subjects for his next two books, published (in collaboration with Lombroso) in 1893 and 1895: *La donna delinquente* (*The Female Offender*) and *Il mondo criminale italiano* (*The Italian Criminal World*).

Traveling to England in 1893, Ferrero made contacts in the British Labour movement. Back in Turin in 1894 he was put on trial as part of a government move to repress socialist organizations and sentenced to two months *domicilio coatto* (home detention) to be served at Oulx, high in the Val de Susa. But he was allowed to postpone serving this sentence until after another journey, this time to Berlin, Moscow (where he met Leo Tolstoy), and Scandinavia. Returning to his confinement at Oulx, he wrote in the spring of 1897 *L'Europa giovane* (*Young Europe*), outlining how young people could contribute to the potential he saw for Europe in the coming century. His earlier books had gained some attention, for instance because of the attempt in *La donna delinquente* to expound a link between cranial measurement and criminality in women, which had piqued public interest; but *L'Europa giovane* touched a highly responsive chord in the public mind and gave Ferrero the status of an intellectual hero: a status which he never lost.

Confidence in his ability bore Ferrero over the misgivings others felt when he turned his attention to the ancient world. "When I expressed my intention to write a new history of Rome," he says in this book, "many people manifested a sense of astonishment similar to what they would have felt had I said that I meant to retire to a monastery." Publishers as well as friends "at first showed themselves sceptical and hesitating." Not that the plan was as eccentric as they thought: In 1902, the year when Ferrero's first volume was published, Theodor Mommsen received the Nobel Prize for Literature for his *Römische Geschichte* (*History of Rome*), finished a decade earlier.

Ferrero used ancient Rome "to think with." He records (perhaps conceitedly) an incident at the Collège de France when "an illustrious historian, a member of the French Academy" complimented him, and he replied by saying, "But I have not re-made Roman history, as many admirers think. On the contrary. . .I have only returned to the old way. I have retaken the point of view of Livy; like Livy, gathering the events of the story of Rome around that phenomenon which the ancients called the 'corruption' of customs."

"Corruption" receives enthusiastic exposition in *Characters and Events of Roman History*. Livy's famous sentence is quoted:

> Rome was originally, when it was poor and small, a unique example of austere virtue; then it corrupted, it spoiled, it rotted itself by all the vices; so, little by little, we have been brought into the present condition in which we are able neither to tolerate the evils from which we suffer, nor the remedies we need to cure them.

The near unanimity of Roman voices on this sentiment in their literature, politics and legislation is placed alongside Rome's long-continued success in governing an immense empire. What kind of thing is "corruption," Ferrero asks, if it is something which both provokes that moral reaction and promotes (or at least does not impede) those practical results?

Ferrero's answer, in brief, is that "corruption" is the name the Romans had for what the modern world calls "progress" — the ancient moral objection arose from observing "the historic force that, as riches increase, impels the new generations to desire new satisfactions, new pleasures." This opens a door for moral commentary on twentieth-century life: Ferrero reflects on ancient sumptuary laws as contrasted with modern freedom to consume; on relations between the Western world and the Eastern, parents and children, men and women, the decreasing birth rate. Foreboding seems to overshadow the author's words when he says, "we can boast in the pride of triumph that we are the first who dare in the midst of a conquered world, to enjoy — enjoy without scruple, without restriction — all the good things life offers to the strong."

By writing — really — about the twentieth century, Ferrero implicitly rejected the academic historical study whose greatest nineteenth-century exponent had been Mommsen. Ferrero speaks slightingly of his kind of research as a symptom of the unworldliness of universities: "Roman studies," he says, "feeling the new generations becoming estranged from them, have for the last twenty-five years tended to take refuge in the tranquil cloisters of learning, of archaeology, in the discreet concourse of a few wise men, who voluntarily flee the noises of the world. Fatal thought! Ancient Rome ought to live daily in the mind of the new social classes that lead onward. . . ."

Ferrero's methods as a Roman historian were conservative, based above all on literary texts: the histories written by Romans, and speeches and letters by Roman authors. Hence his interest in Livy, and his inference that what Livy had to say about the moral failings of ancient Rome was worth pondering in the twentieth century. He had a good knowledge of the literature, though his scope was narrow compared to what Edward Gibbon's had been; and he could play the game of critical historical study well enough to make him plausible alongside nineteenth- and twentieth-century researchers when it suited him (as in this book when he demythologizes Antony and Cleopatra, and argues that "the Tiberius of Tacitus and Suetonius is a fantastic personality, the hero of a wretched and improbable romance, invented by party hatred"), but his essential project was prophetic rather than critical.

Prophetic, however, not always in the way one might expect from a left-wing author. Ferrero himself stressed that "my work does not belong among those written after the method of economic materialism," (the perspective typical of Marxist historical work) "for I hold that the fundamental force in history is psychologic and not economic." He used certain bits of vocabulary characteristic of socialist work—for instance describing Nero as "the victim of the contradictory situation of his times," and opining that "if history in its details is a continuous strife, as a whole it is the inevitable final reconciliation of antagonistic forces, obtained in spite of the resistance of individuals and by sacrificing them." There speaks Ferrero the pre-First World War, pre-Russian Revolution left-winger: a Ferrero with a Hegelian voice. But he showed another side of his outlook by describing the last chapter in this book as being about "the role which Rome can still play in the education of the upper classes." "History," he says, "can form a kind of wisdom set apart," adding, "in a certain sense aristocratic, above what the masses know, at least as to the universal laws which govern the life of nations." This is hardly what would be expected from an intellectual dedicated to furthering the cause of the proletariat.

Characters and Events of Roman History was received, as Ferrero himself was received in America, with an enthusiasm bordering on the deferential. In the *New York Times* (which had reported his visit, down to reproducing the wire he sent President Roosevelt on sailing from New York), the writer of an unsigned review raises a polite question over the value of the lectures ("standing alone, they are practically undemonstrated conclusions from unformulated premises and have to be accepted more or less on faith"), but adds, "Ferrero is a man big enough to do about as he pleases, and his books must be read, whatever the form in which he chooses to issue them."

The reviewer was perhaps not a hundred percent fair about "undemonstrated conclusions": Ferrero had written with more detail and more scholarly apparatus in *The Greatness and Decline of Rome*, his five-volume history, and a printed lecture is still only a lecture. Yet his reaction shows something about the way nineteenth-century research universities in Europe and America had changed the rules of intellectual engagement by 1908. Among academic historians of Rome, though Ferrero was accorded the respect due to an intellectual giant (given honorary doctorates, invited to speak in famous universities), he was not seen as being engaged in the pursuit of quite the same goals as the academics. Nobel-prize-winner Mommsen had begun his scientific career with several years in Italy studying Latin inscriptions—a labour which brought about vast additions to modern knowledge of Roman constitutional law. Where Mommsen had been a researcher, Ferrero was a popularizer.

Late in life, however, fate was to bring Ferrero into the academic career he decided against in youth. After Mussolini's 1922 coup, *Il secolo* changed its editorial line from radical to pro-Fascist, and Ferrero's association with the paper came to an end. Before long he published *Da Fiume a Roma*, translated into English as *Four Years of Fascism* (1924). Much of the space is occupied by reprinted newspaper columns (Ferrero does not name the paper in which they appeared). The author's vigorous anti-Fascist stance is clear. In 1925 Ferrero's passport was withdrawn, and he was threatened with imprisonment and put under police surveillance. During the following years he lived in the countryside and worked on a four-volume novel, *La terza Roma* (*The Third Rome*). In October 1929 Mussolini personally refused to allow Ferrero a passport; later he modified his stance by deciding to give Ferrero a passport but not allow passports to be given to his family. But in February 1930 the University of Geneva invited Ferrero to a conference; and the intervention of the king of Belgium induced the Fascist government to allow Gina Ferrero to accompany her husband.

Asked to accept a university appointment in Geneva, Ferrero joined the *Institut universitaire de hautes études internationales* (University of Geneva Institute for Advanced International Studies) as a professor of contemporary history. To the disappointment of colleagues, but perhaps wisely, he declined to teach ancient history. His courses in the Institute attracted few ordinary students, but gained plenty of local and international public attention — that was the value the University gained by employing him. He lived and worked in Geneva until his death in 1942. His last two courses were published in America, in French, as *Histoire analytique de la révolution française*, after the 1940 fall of France.

Paul McKechnie is a Senior Lecturer in Classics and Ancient History in the University of Auckland, New Zealand. He is the author of *The First Christian Centuries* (2001).

PREFACE

In the spring of 1906, the Collège de France invited me to deliver, during November of that year, a course of lectures on Roman history. I accepted, giving a résumé, in eight lectures, of the history of the government of Augustus from the end of the civil wars to his death; that is, a résumé of the matter contained in the fourth and fifth volumes of the English edition of my work, *The Greatness and Decline of Rome.*

Following these lectures came a request from M. Emilio Mitre, Editor of the chief newspaper of the Argentine Republic, the *Nacion,* and one from the *Academia Brazileira de Lettras* of Rio de Janeiro, to deliver a course of lectures in the Argentine and Brazilian capitals. I gave to the South American course a more general character than that delivered in Paris, introducing arguments which would interest a public having a less specialized knowledge of history than the public I had addressed in Paris.

When President Roosevelt did me the honour to invite me to visit the United States and Prof. Abbott Lawrence Lowell asked me to deliver a course at the Lowell Institute in Boston, I selected material from the two previous courses of lectures, moulding it into the group that was given in Boston in November-December, 1908. These lectures were later read at Columbia University in New York, and at the University of Chicago in Chicago. Certain of them were delivered elsewhere—before the American Philosophical Society and at the University of Pennsylvania in Philadelphia, at Harvard University in Cambridge, and at Cornell University in Ithaca.

Such is the record of the book now presented to the public at large. It is a work necessarily made up of detached studies, which, however, are bound together by a central, unifying thought; so that the reading of them may prove useful and pleasant even to those who have already read my *Greatness and Decline of Rome.*

The first lecture, "The Theory of Corruption in Roman History," sums up the fundamental idea of my conception of the history of Rome. The essential phenomenon upon which all the political, social, and moral crises of Rome depend is the transformation of customs produced by the augmentation of wealth, of expenditure, and of needs,—a phenomenon, therefore, of psychological order, and one common in contemporary life. This lecture should show that my work does not belong among those written after the method of economic materialism, for I hold that the fundamental force in history is psychologic and not economic.

The three following lectures, "The History and Legend of Antony and Cleopatra," "The Development of Gaul," and "Nero," seem to concern themselves with very different subjects. On the contrary, they present three different aspects of the one, identical problem—the struggle between the Occident and the Orient—a problem that Rome succeeded in solving as no European civilisation has since been able to do, making the countries of the Mediterranean Basin share a common life, in peace. How Rome succeeded in accomplishing this union of Orient and Occident is one of the points of greatest interest in its history. The first of these three lectures, "Antony and Cleopatra," shows how Rome repulsed the last offensive movement of the Orient against the Occident; the second, "The Development of Gaul," shows the establishing of equilibrium between the two parts of the Empire; the third, "Nero," shows how the Orient, beaten upon fields of battle and in diplomatic action, took its revenge in the domain of Roman ideas, morals, and social life.

The fifth lecture, "Julia and Tiberius," illustrates, by one of the most tragic episodes of Roman history, the terrible struggle between Roman ideals and habits and those of the Græco-Asiatic civilisation. The sixth lecture, "The Development of the Empire," summarises in a few pages views to be developed in detail in that part of my work yet to be written.

I have said that not all history can be explained by economic forces and factors, but this does not prevent me from regarding economic phenomena as also of high importance. The seventh lecture, "Wine in Roman History," is an essay after the plan in accordance with which, it seems to me, economic phenomena should be treated.

The last lecture deals with a subject that perhaps does not, properly speaking, belong to Roman history, but upon which an historian of Rome ought to touch sooner or later; I mean the rôle which Rome can still play in the education of the upper classes. It is a subject important not only to the historian of Rome, but to all those who are interested in the future of culture and civilisation. The more specialisation in technical labour increases, the greater becomes the necessity of giving the superior classes a general education, which can prepare specialists to understand each other and to act together in all matters of common interest. To imagine a society composed exclusively of doctors, engineers, chemists, merchants, and manufacturers is impossible. Every one must also be a citizen and a man in sympathy with the common conscience. I have, therefore, endeavoured to show in this eighth lecture what services Rome and its great intellectual tradition can render to modern civilisation in the field of education.

These lectures naturally cannot do more than make known ideas in general form; it would be too much to expect in them the precision of detail, the regard for method, and the use of frequent notes, citations, and references to authorities or documents, that belong to my larger work on Rome; but they are published partly because I consider it useful to popularise Roman history, and partly because some of the pleasantest of memories attach to them. Their origin, the course on Augustus given at the Collège de France, which proved one of the happiest occasions of my life, and their development, leading to my travels in the two Americas, have given me experiences of the greatest interest and pleasure.

I am glad of the opportunity here to thank all those who have contributed to make the sojourn of my wife and myself in the United States delightful. I must thank all my friends at once; for to name each one separately, I should need, as a Latin poet says, "a hundred mouths and a hundred tongues."

GUGLIELMO FERRERO.

TURIN, February 22, 1909.

"CORRUPTION" IN ANCIENT ROME
AND ITS COUNTERPART
IN MODERN HISTORY

Two years ago in Paris, while giving a course of lectures on Augustus at the Collège de France, I happened to say to an illustrious historian, a member of the French Academy, who was complimenting me: "But I have not re-made Roman history, as many admirers think. On the contrary, it might be said, in a certain sense, that I have only returned to the old way. I have retaken the point of view of Livy; like Livy, gathering the events of the story of Rome around that phenomenon which the ancients called the 'corruption' of customs—a novelty twenty centuries old!"

Spoken with a smile and in jest, these words nevertheless were more serious than the tone in which they were uttered. All those who know Latin history and literature, even superficially, remember with what insistence and with how many diverse modulations of tone are reiterated the laments on the corruption of customs, on the luxury, the ambition, the avarice, that invaded Rome after the Second Punic War. Sallust, Cicero, Livy, Horace, Virgil, are full of affliction because Rome is destined to dissipate itself in an incurable corruption; whence we see, then in Rome, as to-day in France, wealth, power, culture, glory, draw in their train—grim but inseparable comrade!—a pessimism that times poorer, cruder, more troubled, had not known. In the very moment in which the empire was ordering itself, civil wars ended; in that solemn *Pax Romana* which was to have endured so many ages, in the very moment in which the heart should have opened itself to hope and

1

to joy, Horace describes, in three fine, terrible verses, four successive generations, each corrupting Rome, which grew ever the worse, ever the more perverse and evil-disposed:

> Ætas parentum, peior avis, tulit
> Nos requiores, mox laturos
> Progeniem vitiosiorem.

"Our fathers were worse than our grandsires; we have deteriorated from our fathers; our sons will cause *us* to be lamented." This is the dark philosophy that a sovereign spirit like Horace derived from the incredible triumph of Rome in the world. At his side, Livy, the great writer who was to teach all future generations the story of the city, puts the same hopeless philosophy at the base of his wonderful work:

> Rome was originally, when it was poor and small, a unique example of austere virtue; then it corrupted, it spoiled, it rotted itself by all the vices; so, little by little, we have been brought into the present condition in which we are able neither to tolerate the evils from which we suffer, nor the remedies we need to cure them.

The same dark thought, expressed in a thousand forms, is found in almost every one of the Latin writers.

This theory has misled and impeded my predecessors in different ways: some, considering that the writers bewail the unavoidable dissolution of Roman society at the very time when Rome was most powerful, most cultured, richest, have judged conventional, rhetorical, literary, these invectives against corruption, these praises of ancient simplicity, and therefore have held them of no value in the history of Rome. Such critics have not reflected that this conception is found, not only in the literature, but also in the politics and the legislation; that Roman history is full, not only of invectives in prose and verse, but of laws and administrative provisions against *luxuria, ambitio, avaritia*—a sign that these laments were not merely a foolishness of writers, or, as we say to-day, stuff for newspaper articles. Other critics, instead, taking account of these laws and administrative provisions, have accepted the ancient theory of Roman corruption without reckoning that they were describing as undone by an irreparable dissolution, a nation that not only had conquered, but was to govern for ages, an immense empire. In this conception of corruption there is a contradiction that conceals a great universal problem.

Stimulated by this contradiction, and by the desire of solving it, to study more attentively the facts cited by the ancients as examples of corruption, I have looked about to see if in the contemporary world I could not find some things that resembled it, and so make myself understand it. The prospect seemed difficult, because modern men are persuaded that they are models of all the virtues. Who could think to find in them even traces of the famous Roman corruption? In the modern world to-day are the abominable orgies carried on for which the Rome of the Cæsars was notorious? Are there to-day Neros and Elagabaluses? He who studies the ancient sources, however, with but a little of the critical spirit, is easily convinced that we have made for ourselves out of the much-famed corruption and Roman luxury a notion highly romantic and exaggerated. We need not delude ourselves: Rome, even in the times of its greatest splendour, was poor in comparison with the modern world; even in the second century after Christ, when it stood as metropolis at the head of an immense empire, Rome was smaller, less wealthy, less imposing, than a great metropolis of Europe or of America. Some sumptuous public edifices, beautiful private houses —that is all the splendour of the metropolis of the empire. He who goes to the Palatine may to-day refigure for himself, from the so-called House of Livia, the house of a rich Roman family of the time of Augustus, and convince himself that a well-to-do middle-class family would hardly occupy such a house to-day.

Moreover, the palaces of the Cæsars on the Palatine are a grandiose ruin that stirs the artist and makes the philosopher think; but if one sets himself to measure them, to conjecture from the remains the proportions of the entire edifices, he does not con-

3

jure up buildings that rival large modern constructions. The palace of Tiberius, for example, rose above a street only two metres wide —less than seven feet,—an alley like those where to-day in Italian cities live only the most miserable inhabitants. We have pictured to ourselves the imperial banquets of ancient Rome as functions of unheard of splendour; if Nero or Elagabalus could come to life and see the dining-room of a great hotel in Paris or New York— resplendent with light, with crystal, with silver,—he would admire it as far more beautiful than the halls in which he gave his imperial feasts. Think how poor were the ancients in artificial light! They had few wines; they knew neither tea nor coffee nor cocoa; neither tobacco, nor the innumerable *liqueurs* of which we make use; in face of our habits, they were always Spartan, even when they wasted, because they lacked the means to squander.

The ancient writers often lament the universal tendency to physical self-indulgence, but among the facts they cite to prove this dismal vice, many would seem to us innocent enough. It was judged by them a scandalous proof of gluttony and as insensate luxury, that at a certain period there should be fetched from as far as the Pontus, certain sausages and certain salted fish that were, it appears, very good; and that there should be introduced into Italy from Greece the delicate art of fattening fowls. Even to drink Greek wines seemed for a long time at Rome the caprice of an almost crazy luxury. As late as 18 B.C., Augustus made a sumptuary law that forbade spending for banquets on work-days more than two hundred sesterces (ten dollars); allowed three hundred sesterces (fifteen dollars) for the days of the Kalends, the Ides, and the Nones; and one thousand sesterces (fifty dollars) for nuptial banquets. It is clear, then, that the lords of the world banqueted in state at an expense that to us would seem modest indeed. And the women of ancient times, accused so sharply by the men of ruining them by their foolish extravagances, would cut a poor figure for elegant ostentation in comparison with modern dames of fashion. For example, silk, even in the most prosperous times, was considered a stuff, as we should say, for millionaires; only a few very rich women wore it; and, moreover, moralists detested it, because it revealed too clearly the form of the body. Lollia Paulina passed into history because she possessed jewels worth several million francs: there are to-day too many Lollia Paulinas for any one of them to hope to buy immortality at so cheap a rate.

I should reach the same conclusions if I could show you what the Roman writers really meant by corruption in their accounts of the relations between the sexes. It is not possible here to make critical analyses of texts and facts concerning this material, for reasons that you readily divine; but it would be easy to prove that also in this respect posterity has seen the evil much larger than it was.

Why, then, did the ancient writers bewail luxury, inclination to pleasure, prodigality — things all comprised in the notorious "corruption" — in so much the livelier fashion than do moderns, although they lived in a world which, being poorer and more simple, could amuse itself, make display, and indulge in dissipation so much less than we do? This is one of the chief questions of Roman history, and I flatter myself not to have entirely wasted work in writing my book[1]; above all, because I hope to have contributed a little, if not actually to solve this question, at least to illuminate it; because in so doing I believe I have found a kind of key that opens at the same time many mysteries in Roman history and in contemporary life. The ancient writers and moralists wrote so much of Roman corruption, because — nearer in this, as in so many other things, to the vivid actuality — they understood that wars, revolutions, the great spectacular events that are accomplished in sight of the world, do not form all the life of peoples; that these occurrences, on the contrary, are but the ultimate, exterior explanation, the external irradiation, or the final explosion of an internal force that is acting constantly in the family, in private habit, in the moral and intellectual disposition of the individual. They understood that all the changes, internal and external, in a nation, are bound together and in part depend on one very common fact, which is everlasting and universal, and which everybody may observe if he will but look about him—on the increase of wants, the enlargement of ideas, the shifting of habits, the advance of luxury, the increase of expense that is caused by every generation.

Look around you to-day: in every family you may easily observe the same phenomenon. A man has been born in a certain social condition and has succeeded during his youth and vigour in adding to his original fortune. Little by little as he was growing rich, his needs and his luxuries increased. When a certain point was reached, he stopped. The men are few who can indefinitely augment their particular wants, or keep changing their habits throughout their lives, even after the disappearance of vigour and virile elasticity. The increase of wants and of luxury, the change of habits, continues, instead, in the new generation, in the children, who began to live in the ease which their fathers won after long effort and fatigue, and in maturer age; who, in short, started where the previous generation left off, and therefore wish to gain yet new enjoyments, different from and greater than those that they obtained without trouble through the efforts of the preceding generation. It is this little common drama, which we see re-enacted in every family and in which every one of us has been and will be an actor—to-day as a young radical who innovates customs, to-morrow as an old conservative, out-of-date and malcontent in the eyes of the young; a drama, petty and common, which no one longer regards, so frequent is it and so frivolous it seems, but which, instead, is one of the greatest motive forces in human history—in greater or less degree, under different forms, active in all times and operating everywhere. On account of it no generation can live quietly on the wealth gathered, with the ideas discovered by antecedent generations, but is constrained to create new ideas, to make new and greater wealth by all the means at its disposal—by war and conquest, by agriculture and industry, by religion and science. On account of it, families, classes, nations, that do not succeed in adding to their possessions, are destined to be impoverished, because, wants increasing, it is necessary, in order to satisfy them, to consume the accumulated capital, to make debts, and, little by little, to go to ruin. Because of this ambition, ever reborn, classes renew themselves in every nation. Opulent families after a few generations are gradually impoverished; they decay and disappear, and from the multitudinous poor arise new families, creating the new *élite* which continues under differing forms the doings and traditions of the old. Because of this unrest, the earth is always stirred up by a fervour for deeds of adventure—attempts that take shape according to the age: now peoples make war on each other, now they rend themselves in revolutions, now they seek new lands, explore, conquer, exploit; again they perfect arts and industries, enlarge commerce, cultivate the earth with greater assiduity; and yet again, in the ages more laborious, like ours, they do all these things at the same time —an activity immense and continuous. But its motive force is always the need of the new generations, that, starting from the point at which their predecessors had arrived, desire to advance yet farther —to enjoy, to know, to possess yet more.

The ancient writers understood this thoroughly: what they called "corruption" was but the change in customs and wants, proceeding from generation to generation, and in its essence the same as that which takes place about us to-day. The *avaritia* of which they complained so much, was the greed and impatience to make money that we see to-day setting all classes beside themselves, from noble to day-labourer; the *ambitio* that appeared to the ancients to animate so frantically even the classes that ought to have been most immune, was what we call *getting there*—the craze to rise at any cost to a condition higher than that in which one was born, which so many writers, moralists, statesmen, judge, rightly or wrongly, to be one of the most dangerous maladies of the modern world. *Luxuria* was the desire to augment personal conveniences, luxuries, pleasures—the same passion that stirs Europe and America to-day from top to bottom, in city and country. Without doubt, wealth grew in ancient Rome and grows to-day; men were bent on making money in the last two centuries of the Republic, and to-day they rush headlong into the delirious struggle for gold; for reasons and motives, however, and with arms and accoutrements, far diverse.

As I have already said, ancient civilisation was narrower, poorer, and more ignorant; it did not hold under its victorious foot the whole earth; it did not possess the formidable instruments with which we exploit the forces and the resources of nature: but the treasures of precious metals transported to Italy from conquered and subjugated countries; the lands, the mines, the forests, belonging to such countries, confiscated by Rome and given or rented to Italians; the tributes imposed on the vanquished, and the collection of them; the abundance of slaves, — all these then offered to the Romans and to the Italians so many occasions to grow rich quickly; just as the gigantic economic progress of the modern world offers similar opportunities to-day to all the peoples that, by geographical position, historical tradition, or vigorous culture and innate energy, know how to excel in industry, in agriculture, and in trade. Especially from the Second Punic War on, in all classes, there followed —anxious for a life more affluent and brilliant—generations the more incited to follow the examples that emanated from the great metropolises of the Orient, particularly Alexandria, which was for the Romans of the Republic what Paris is for us to-day. This movement, spontaneous, regular, natural, was every now and then violently accelerated by the conquest of a great Oriental state. One observes, after each one of the great annexations of Oriental lands, a more intense delirium of luxury and pleasure: the first time, after the acquisition of the kingdom of Pergamus, through a kind of contagion communicated by the sumptuous furniture of King Attalus, which was sold at auction and scattered among the wealthy houses of Italy to excite the still simple desires and the yet sluggish imaginations of the Italians; the second time, after the conquest of Pontus and of Syria, made by Lucullus and by Pompey; finally, the third time, after the conquest of Egypt made by Augustus, when the influence of that land — the France of the ancient world — so actively invaded Italy that no social force could longer resist it.

In this way, partly by natural, gradual, almost imperceptible diffusion, partly by violent crises, we see the mania for luxury and the appetite for pleasure beginning, growing, becoming aggravated from generation to generation in all Roman society, for two centuries, changing the mentality and morality of the people; we see the institutions and public policy being altered; all Roman history a-making under the action of this force, formidable and immanent in the whole nation. It breaks down all obstacles confronting it—the forces of traditions, laws, institutions, interests of classes, opposition of parties, the efforts of thinking men. The historical aristocracy becomes impoverished and weak; before it rise to power the millionaires, the *parvenus*, the great capitalists, enriched in the provinces. A part of the nobility, after having long despised them, sets itself to fraternise with them, to marry their wealthy daughters, cause them to share power; seeks to prop with their millions the preeminence of its own rank, menaced by the discontent, the spirit of revolt, the growing pride, of the middle class. Meanwhile, another part of the aristocracy, either too haughty and ambitious, or too poor, scorns this alliance, puts itself at the head of the democratic party, foments in the middle classes the spirit of antagonism against the nobles and the rich, leads them to the assault on the citadels of aristocratic and democratic power. Hence the mad internal struggles that redden Rome with blood and complicate so tragically, especially after the Gracchi, the external polity. The increasing wants of the members of all classes, the debts that are their inevitable consequence, the universal longing, partly unsatisfied for lack of means, for the pleasures of the subtle Asiatic civilisations, infused into this whole history a demoniac frenzy that to-day, after so many centuries, fascinates and appals us.

To satisfy their wants, to pay their debts, the classes now set upon each other, each to rob in turn the goods of the other, in the cruelest civil war that history records; now, tired of doing themselves evil, they unite and precipitate themselves on the world outside of Italy, to sack the wealth that its owners do not know how to defend. In the great revolutions of Marius and Sulla, the democratic party is the instrument with which a part of the debt-burdened middle classes seek to rehabilitate themselves by robbing the plutocracy and the aristocracy yet opulent; but Sulla reverses the situation, makes a coalition of aristocrats and the miserable of the populace, and re-establishes the fortunes of the nobility, despoiling the wealthy knights and a part of the middle classes—a terrible civil war that leaves in Italy a hate, a despondency, a distress, that seem at a certain moment as if they must weigh eternally on the spirit of the unhappy nation. When, lo! there appears the strongest man in the history of Rome, Lucullus, and drags Italy out of the despondency in which it crouched, leads it into the ways of the world, and persuades it that the best means of forgetting the losses and ruin undergone in the civil wars, is to recuperate on the riches of the cowardly Orientals. As little by little the treasures of Mithridates, conquered by Lucullus in the Orient, arrive in Italy, Italy begins anew to divert itself, to construct palaces and villas, to squander in luxury. Pompey, envious of the glory of Lucullus, follows his example, conquers Syria, sends new treasures to Italy, carries from the East the jewels of Mithridates, and displaying them in the temple of Jove, rouses a passion for gems in the Roman women; he also builds the first great stone theatre to rise in Rome. All the political men in Rome try to make money out of foreign countries: those who cannot, like the great, conquer an empire, confine themselves to blackmailing the countries and petty states that tremble before the shadow of Rome; the courts of the secondary kings of the Orient, the court of the Ptolemies at Alexandria,—all are invaded by a horde of insatiable senators and knights, who, menacing and promising, extort money to spend in Italy and foment the growing extravagance. The debts pile up, the political corruption overflows, scandals follow, the parties in Rome rend each other madly, though hail-fellow-well-met in the provinces to plunder subjects and vassals. In the midst of this vast disorder Cæsar, the man of destiny, rises, and with varying fortune makes a way for himself until he beckons Italy to follow him, to find success and treasures in regions new—not in the rich and fabulous East, but beyond the Alps, in barbarous Gaul, bristling with fighters and forests.

But this insane effort to prey on every part of the Empire finally tires Italy; quarrels over the division of spoils embitter friends; the immensity of the conquests, made in a few years of reckless enthusiasm, is alarming. Finally a new civil war breaks out, terrible and interminable, in which classes and families fall upon each other anew, to tear away in turn the spoils taken together abroad. Out of the tremendous discord rises at last the pacifier, Augustus, who is able gradually, by cleverness and infinite patience, to re-establish peace and order in the troubled empire. How? — why? Because the combination of events of the times allows him to use to ends of peace the same forces with which the preceding generations had fomented so much disorder — desires for ease, pleasure, culture, wealth growing with the generations making it. Thereupon begins in the whole Empire universal progress in agriculture, industry, trade, which, on a small scale, may be compared to what we to-day witness and share; a progress for which, then as now, the chief condition was peace. As soon as men realised that peace gives that greater wealth, those enjoyments more refined, that higher culture, which for a century they had sought by war, Italy became quiet; revolutionists became guardians and guards of order; there gathered about Augustus a coalition of social forces that tended to impose on the Empire, alike on the parts that wished it and those that did not, the *Pax Romana.*

Now all this immense story that fills three centuries, that gathers within itself so many revolutions, so many legislative reforms, so many great men, so many events, tragic and glorious, this vast history that for so many centuries holds the interest of all cultured nations, and that, considered as a whole, seems almost a prodigy, you can, on the track of the old idea of "corruption," explain in its profoundest origins by one small fact, universal, common, of the very simplest — something that every one may observe in the limited circle of his own personal experience, — by that automatic increase of ambitions and desires, with every new generation, which prevents the human world from crystallising in one form, constrains it to continual changes in material make-up as well as in

ideals and moral appearance. In other words, every new generation must, in order to satisfy that part of its aspirations which is
peculiarly and entirely its own, alter, whether little or much, in
one way or another, the condition of the world it entered at birth.
We can then, in our personal experiences every day, verify the universal law of history—a law that can act with greater or less inten-
sity, more or less rapidity, according to times and places, but that
ceases to authenticate itself at no time and in no place.

The United States is subject to that law to-day, as is old Europe,
as will be future generations, and as past ages were. Moreover, to
understand at bottom this phenomenon, which appears to me to
be the soul of all history, it is well to add this consideration: It is
evident that there is a capital difference between our judgment of
this phenomenon and that of the ancients; to them it was a malev-
olent force of dissolution to which should be attributed all in
Roman history that was sinister and dreadful, a sure sign of incurable decay; that is why they called it "corruption of customs," and
so lamented it. To-day, on the contrary, it appears to us a universal
beneficent process of transformation; so true is this that we call
"progress" many facts which the ancients attributed to "corruption." It were useless to expand too much in examples; enough to
cite a few. In the third ode of the first book, in which he so ten-
derly salutes the departing Virgil, Horace covers with invective, as
an evil-doer and the corrupter of the human race, that impious
being who invented the ship, which causes man, created for the
land, to walk across waters. Who would to-day dare repeat those
maledictions against the bold builders who construct the magnificent trans-Atlantic liners on which, in a dozen days from Genoa,
one lands in Boston or New York? "Cœlum ipsum petimus stulti-
tia," exclaims Horace—that is to say, in anticipation he considered
the Wright brothers crazy.

Who, save some man of erudition, has knowledge to-day of
sumptuary laws? We should laugh them all down with one Homeric
guffaw, if to-day it entered somebody's head to propose a law that
forbade fair ladies to spend more than a certain sum on their

clothes, or numbered the hats they might wear; or that regulated dinners of ceremony, fixing the number of courses, the variety of wines, and the total expense; or that prohibited labouring men and women from wearing certain stuffs or certain objects that were wont to be found only upon the persons of people of wealth and leisure. And yet laws of this tenor were compiled, published, observed, up to two centuries ago, without any one's finding it absurd. The historic force that, as riches increase, impels the new generations to desire new satisfactions, new pleasures, operated then as to-day; only then men were inclined to consider it as a new kind of ominous disease that needed checking. To-day men regard that constant transformation either as beneficent, or at least as such a matter of course that almost no one heeds it; just as no one notices the alternations of day and night, or the change of seasons. On the contrary, we have little by little become so confident of the goodness of this force that drives the coming generation on into the unknown future, that society, European, American, among other liberties has won in the nineteenth century, full and entire, a liberty that the ancients did not know—freedom in vice.

To the Romans it appeared most natural that the state should survey private habits, should spy out what a citizen, particularly a citizen belonging to the ruling classes, did within domestic walls— should see whether he became intoxicated, whether he were a gourmand, whether he contracted debts, spending much or little, whether he betrayed his wife. The age of Augustus was cultured, civilised, liberal, and in many things resembled our own; yet on this point the dominating ideas were so different from ours, that at one time Augustus was forced by public opinion to propose a law on adultery by which all Roman citizens of both sexes guilty of this crime were condemned to exile and the confiscation of half their substance, and there was given to any citizen the right to accuse the guilty. Could you imagine it possible to-day, even for a few weeks, to establish this régime of terror in the kingdom of Amor? But the ancients were always inclined to consider as exceedingly dangerous for the upper classes that relaxing of customs which always follows periods of rapid enrichment, of great gain in comforts; behind his own walls to-day, every one is free to indulge himself as he will, to the confines of crime.

How can we explain this important difference in judging one of the essential phenomena of historic life? Has this phenomenon changed nature, and from bad, by some miracle, become good? Or are we wiser than our forefathers, judging with experience what they could hardly comprehend? There is no doubt that the Latin writers, particularly Horace and Livy, were so severe in condemning this progressive movement of wants because of unconscious political solicitude, because intellectual men expressed the opinions, sentiments, and also the prejudices of historic aristocracy, and this detested the progress of *ambitio, avaritia, luxuria,* because they undermined the dominance of its class. On the other hand, it is certain that in the modern world every increase of consumption, every waste, every vice, seems permissible, indeed almost meritorious, because men of industry and trade, the employees in industries—that is, all the people that gain by the diffusion of luxuries, by the spread of vices or new wants—have acquired, thanks above all to democratic institutions, and to the progress of cities, an immense political power that in times past they lacked. If, for example, in Europe the beer-makers and distillers of alcohol were not more powerful in the electoral field than the philosophers and academicians, governments would more easily recognise that the masses should not be allowed to poison themselves or future generations by chronic drunkenness.

Between these two extremes of exaggeration, inspired by a self-interest easy to discover, is there not a true middle way that we can deduce from the study of Roman history and from the observation of contemporary life?

In the pessimism with which the ancients regarded progress as corruption, there was a basis of truth, just as there is a principle of error in the too serene optimism with which we consider corruption as progress. This force that pushes the new generations on to the future, at once creates and destroys; its destructive energy is specially felt in ages like Cæsar's in ancient Rome and ours in the modern world, in which facility in the accumulation of wealth over-excites desires and ambitions in all classes. They are the times in which personal egoism—what to-day we call individualism—usurps a place above all that represents in society the interest of the species: national duty, the self-abnegation of each for the sake of the common good. Then these vices and defects become always more common: intellectual agitation, the weakening of the spirit of tradition, the general relaxation of discipline, the loss of authority, ethical confusion and disorder. At the same time that certain moral sentiments refine themselves, certain individualisms grow fiercer. The government may no longer represent the ideas, the aspirations, the energetic will of a small oligarchy; it must make itself more yielding and gracious at the same time that it is becoming more contradictory and discordant. Family discipline is relaxed; the new generations shake off early the influence of the past; the sentiment of honour and the rigour of moral, religious, and political principles are weakened by a spirit of utility and expediency by which, more or less openly, confessing it or dissimulating, men always seek to do, not that which is right and decorous, but that which is utilitarian. The civic spirit tends to die out; the number of persons capable of suffering, or even of working, disinterestedly for the common good, for the future, diminishes; children are not wanted; men prefer to live in accord with those in power, ignoring their vices, rather than openly opposing them. Public events do not interest unless they include a personal advantage.

This is the state of mind that is now diffusing itself throughout Europe; the same state of mind that, with the documents at hand, I have found in the age of Cæsar and Augustus, and seen progressively diffusing itself throughout ancient Italy. The likeness is so great that we re-find in those far-away times, especially in the upper classes, exactly that restless condition that we define by the word "nervousness." Horace speaks of this state of mind, which we consider peculiar to ourselves, and describes it, by felicitous image, as *strenua inertia*—strenuous inertia,—agitation vain and ineffective, always wanting something new, but not really knowing what, desiring most ardently yet speedily tiring of a desire gratified. Now it is clear that if these vices spread too much, if they are not complemented by an increase of material resources, of knowledge, of sufficient population, they can lead a nation rapidly to ruin. We do not feel very keenly the fear of this danger—the European-American civilisation is so rich, has at its disposal so much knowledge, so many men, so many instrumentalities, has cut off for itself such a measureless part of the globe, that it can afford to look unafraid into the future. The abyss is so far away that only a few philosophers barely descry it in the gray mist of distant years. But the ancient world—so much poorer, smaller, weaker—felt that it could not squander as we do, and saw the abyss near at hand.

To-day men and women waste fabulous wealth in luxury; that is, they spend not to satisfy some reasonable need, but to show to others of their kind how rich they are, or, further, to make others believe them richer than they are. If these resources were everywhere saved as they are in France, the progress of the world would be quicker, and the new countries would more easily find in Europe and in themselves the capital necessary for their development. At all events, our age develops fast, and notwithstanding all this waste, abounds in a plenty that is enough to keep men from fearing the growth of this wanton luxury and from planning to restrain it by laws. In the ancient world, on the other hand, the wealthy classes and the state had only to abandon themselves a little too much to the prodigality that for us has become almost a regular thing, when suddenly means were wanting to meet the most essential needs of social life. Tacitus has summarised an interesting discourse of Tiberius, in which the famous emperor censures the ladies of Rome in terms cold, incisive, and succinct, because they spend too much money on pearls and diamonds. "Our money," said Tiberius, "goes away to India and we are in want of the precious metals to carry on the military administration; we have to give up the defence of the frontiers." According to the opinion of an administrator so sagacious and a general so valiant as Tiberius, in the richest period of the Roman Empire, a lady of Rome could not buy pearls and diamonds without directly weakening the defence of the frontiers. Indulgence in the luxury of jewels looked almost like high treason.

Similar observations might be made on another grave question —the increase of population. One of the most serious effects of individualism that accompanies the increase of civilisation and wealth, is the decrease of the birth-rate. France, which knows how to temper its luxury, which gives to other peoples an example of saving means for the future, has on the other hand given the example of egoism in the family, lowering the birth-rate. England, for a long time so fecund, seems to follow France. The more uniformly settled and well-to-do parts of the North American Union, the Eastern States and New England, are even more sterile than France. However, no one of these nations suffers to-day from the small increase of population; there are yet so many poor and fecund peoples that they can easily fill the gaps. In the ancient world this was not the case; population was always and everywhere so scanty that if for some reason it diminished but slightly, the states could not get on, finding themselves at the mercy of what they called a "famine of men," a malady more serious and troublesome than over-population. In the Roman Empire the Occidental provinces finally fell into the hands of the barbarians, chiefly because the Græco-Latin civilisation sterilised the family, reducing the population incurably. No wonder that the ancients applied the term "corruption" to a momentum of desires which, although increasing culture and the refinements of living, easily menaced the sources of the nation's physical existence.

There is, then, a more general conclusion to draw from this experience. It is not by chance, nor the unaccountable caprice of a few ancient writers, that we possess so many small facts on the development of luxury and the transformation of customs in ancient Rome; that, for example, among the records of great wars, of diplomatic missions, of catastrophes political and economic, we find given the date when the art of fattening fowls was imported into Italy. The little facts are not so unworthy of the majesty of Roman history as one at first might think. Everything is bound together in the life of a nation, and nothing without importance; the humblest acts, most personal and deepest hidden in the *penetralia* of the home, that no one sees, none knows, have an effect, immediate or remote, on the common life of the nation. There is, between these small, insignificant facts and the wars, the revolutions, the tremendous political and social events that bewilder men, a tie, often invisible to most people, yet nevertheless indestructible.

Nothing in the world is without import: what women spend for their toilet, the resistance that men make from day to day to the temptations of the commonest pleasures, the new and petty needs that insinuate themselves unconsciously into the habits of all; the reading, the conversations, the impressions, even the most fugacious that pass in our spirit—all these things, little and innumerable, that no historian registers, have contributed to produce this revolution, that war, this catastrophe, that political overturn, which men wonder at and study as a prodigy.

The causes of how many apparently mysterious historical events would be more clearly and profoundly known, of how many periods would the spirit be better understood, did we only possess the private records of the families that make up the ruling classes! Every deed we do in the intimacy of the home reacts on the whole of our environment. With our every act we assume a responsibility toward the nation and posterity, the sanction for which, near or far away, is in events. This justifies, at least in part, the ancient conception by which the state had the right to exercise vigilance over its citizens, their private acts, customs, pleasures, vices, caprices. This vigilance, the laws that regulated it, the moral and political teachings that brought pressure to bear in the exercise of these laws, tended above all to charge upon the individual man the social responsibility of his single acts; to remind him that in the things most personal, aside from the individual pain or pleasure, there was an interest, a good or an evil, in common.

Modern men—and it is a revolution greater than that finished in political form in the nineteenth century—have been freed from these bonds, from these obligations. Indeed, modern civilisation has made it a duty for each one to spend, to enjoy, to waste as much as he can, without any disturbing thought as to the ultimate consequences of what he does. The world is so rich, population grows so rapidly, civilisation is armed with so much knowledge in its struggle against the barbarian and against nature, that to-day we are able to laugh at the timid prudence of our forefathers, who had, as it were, a fear of wealth, of pleasure, of love; we can boast in the pride of triumph that we are the first who dare in the midst of a conquered world, to enjoy—enjoy without scruple, without restriction—all the good things life offers to the strong.

But who knows? Perhaps this felicitous moment will not last forever; perhaps one day will see men, grown more numerous, feel the need of the ancient wisdom and prudence. It is at least permitted the philosopher and the historian to ask if this magnificent but unbridled freedom which we enjoy suits all times, and not only those in which nations coming into being can find a small dower in their cradle as you have done—three millions of square miles of land!

THE HISTORY AND LEGEND OF
ANTONY AND CLEOPATRA

IN the history of Rome figures of women are rare, because only men dominated there, imposing everywhere the brute force, the roughness, and the egoism that lie at the base of their nature: they honoured the *mater familias* because she bore children and kept the slaves from stealing the flour from the bin and drinking the wine from the *amphore* on the sly. They despised the woman who made of her beauty and vivacity an adornment of social life, a prize sought after and disputed by the men. However, in this virile history there does appear, on a sudden, the figure of a woman, strange and wonderful, a kind of living Venus. Plutarch thus describes the arrival of Cleopatra at Tarsus and her first meeting with Antony:

She was sailing tranquilly along the Cydnus, on a bark with a golden stern, with sails of purple and oars of silver, and the dip of the oars was rythmed to the sound of flutes, blending with music of lyres. She herself, the Queen, wondrously clad as Venus is pictured, was lying under an awning gold embroidered. Boys dressed as Cupids stood at her side, gently waving fans to refresh her; her maidens, every one beautiful and clad as a Naiad or a Grace, directed the boat, some at the rudder, others at the ropes. Both banks of the stream were sweet with the perfumes burning on the vessel.

Posterity is yet dazzled by this ship, refulgent with purple and gold and melodious with flutes and lyres. If we are spellbound by Plutarch's description, it does not seem strange to us that Antony should be—he who could not only behold in person that wonderful Venus, but could dine with her *tête-à-tête*, in a splendour of torches indescribable. Surely this is a setting in no wise improbable for the beginning of the famous romance of the love of Antony and Cleopatra, and its development as probable as its beginning; the follies committed by Antony for the seductive Queen of the Orient, the divorce of Octavia, the war for love of Cleopatra, kindled in the whole Empire, and the miserable catastrophe. Are there not to be seen in recent centuries many men of power putting their greatness to risk and sometimes to ruin for love of a woman? Are not the love letters of great statesmen—for instance, those of Mirabeau and of Gambetta—admitted to the semi-official part of modern history-writing? And so also Antony could love a queen and, like so many modern statesmen, commit follies for her. A French critic of my book, burning his ships behind him, has said that Antony was a Roman *Boulanger.*

The romance pleases: art takes it as subject and re-takes it; but that does not keep off the brutal hands of criticism. Before all, it should be observed that moderns feel and interpret the romance of Antony and Cleopatra in a way very different from that of the ancients. From Shakespeare to De Heredia and Henri Houssaye, artists and historians have described with sympathy, even almost idealised, this passion that throws away in a lightning flash every human greatness, to pursue the mantle of a fleeing woman; they find in the follies of Antony something profoundly human that moves them, fascinates them, and makes them indulgent. To the ancients, on the contrary, the *amours* of Antony and Cleopatra were but a dishonourable degeneration of the passion. They have no excuse for the man whom love for a woman impelled to desert in battle, to abandon soldiers, friends, relatives, to conspire against the greatness of Rome.

This very same difference of interpretation recurs in the history of the *amours* of Cæsar. Modern writers regard what the ancients tell us of the numerous loves—real or imaginary—of Cæsar, as almost a new laurel with which to decorate his figure.

On the contrary, the ancients recounted and spread abroad, and perhaps in part invented, these storiettes of gallantry for quite opposite reasons—as source of dishonour, to discredit him, to demonstrate that Cæsar was effeminate, that he could not give guarantee of knowing how to lead the armies and to fulfil the virile and arduous duties that awaited every eminent Roman. There is in our way of thinking a vein of romanticism wanting in the ancient mind. We see in love a certain forgetfulness of ourselves, a certain blindness of egoism and the more material passions, a kind of power of self-abnegation, which, inasmuch as it is unconscious, confers a certain nobility and dignity; therefore we are indulgent to mistakes and follies committed for the sake of passion, while the ancients were very severe. We pardon with a certain compassion the man who for love of a woman has not hesitated to bury himself under the ruin of his own greatness; the ancients, on the contrary, considered him the most dangerous and despicable of the insane.

Criticism has not contented itself with re-giving to the ancient romance the significance it had for those that made it and the public that first read it. Archæologists have discovered upon coins portraits of Cleopatra, and now critics have confronted these portraits with the poetic descriptions given by Roman historians and have found the descriptions generously fanciful: in the portraits we do not see the countenance of a Venus, delicate, gracious, smiling, nor even the fine and sensuous beauty of a Marquise de Pompadour, but a face fleshy and, as the French would say, *bouffie;* the nose, a powerful aquiline; the face of a woman on in years, ambitious, imperious, one which recalls that of Maria Theresa. It will be said that judgments as to beauty are personal; that Antony, who saw her alive, could decide better than we who see her portraits half effaced by the centuries; that the attractive power of a woman emanates not only from corporal beauty, but also—and yet more—from her spirit. The taste of Cleopatra, her vivacity, her cleverness, her exquisite art in conversation, is vaunted by all.

Perhaps, however, Cleopatra, beautiful or ugly, is of little consequence; when one studies the history of her relations with
Antony, there is small place, and that but toward the end, for the
passion of love. It will be easy to persuade you of this if you follow
the simple chronological exposition of facts I shall give you.
Antony makes the acquaintance of Cleopatra at Tarsus toward the
end of 41 B.C., passes the winter of 41–40 with her at Alexandria;
leaves her in the spring of 40 and stays away from her more than
three years, till the autumn of 37. There is no proof that during
this time Antony sighed for the Queen of Egypt as a lover far
away; on the contrary, he attends, with alacrity worthy of praise, to
preparing the conquest of Persia, to putting into execution the
great design conceived by Cæsar, the plan of war that Antony had
come upon among the papers of the Dictator the evening of the
fifteenth of March, 44 B.C. All order social and political, the
army, the state, public finance, wealth private and public, is
going to pieces around him. The triumvirate power, built up on
the uncertain foundation of these ruins, is tottering; Antony
realises that only a great external success can give to him and his
party the authority and the money necessary to establish a solid
government, and resolves to enter into possession of the political
legacy of his teacher and patron, taking up its central idea, the
conquest of Persia.

The difficulties are grave. Soldiers are not wanting, but money.
The revolution has ruined the Empire and Italy; all the reserve
funds have been dissipated; the finances of the state are in such
straits that not even the soldiers can be paid punctually and the
legions every now and then claim their dues by revolt. Antony is not
discouraged. The historians, however antagonistic to him, describe
him as exceedingly busy in those four years, extracting from all
parts of the Empire that bit of money still in circulation. Then at
one stroke, in the second half of 37, when, preparations finished, it
is time to put hand to the execution, the ancient historians without
in any way explaining to us this sudden act, most unforeseen, make
him depart for Antioch to meet Cleopatra, who has been invited by

him to join him. For what reason does Antony after three years, all of a sudden, re-join Cleopatra? The secret of the story of Antony and Cleopatra lies entirely in this question.

Plutarch says that Antony went to Antioch borne by the fiery and untamed courser of his own spirit; in other words, because passion was already beginning to make him lose common sense. Not finding other explanations in the ancient writers, posterity has accepted this, which was simple enough; but about a century ago an erudite Frenchman, Letronne, studying certain coins, and comparing with them certain passages in ancient historians, until then remaining obscure, was able to demonstrate that in 36 B.C., at Antioch, Antony married Cleopatra with all the dynastic ceremonies of Egypt, and that thereupon Antony became King of Egypt, although he did not dare assume the title.

The explanation of Letronne, which is founded on official documents and coins, is without doubt more dependable than that of Plutarch, which is reducible to an imaginative metaphor; and the discovery of Letronne, concluding that concatenation of facts that I have set forth, finally persuades me to affirm that not a passion of love, suddenly re-awakened, led Antony in the second half of 37 B.C. to Antioch to meet the Queen of Egypt, but a political scheme well thought out. Antony wanted Egypt and not the beautiful person of its queen; he meant by this dynastic marriage to establish the Roman protectorate in the valley of the Nile, and to be able to dispose, for the Persian campaign, of the treasures of the Kingdom of the Ptolemies. At that time, after the plunderings of other regions of the Orient by the politicians of Rome, there was but one state rich in reserves of precious metals, Egypt. Since, little by little, the economic crisis of the Roman Empire was aggravating, the Roman polity had to gravitate perforce toward Egypt, as toward the country capable of providing Rome with the capital necessary to continue its policy in every part of the Empire.

Cæsar already understood this; his mysterious and obscure connection with Cleopatra had certainly for ultimate motive and reason this political necessity; and Antony, in marrying Cleopatra, probably only applied more or less shrewdly the ideas that Cæsar had originated in the refulgent crepuscle of his tempestuous career. You will ask me why Antony, if he had need of the valley of the Nile, recurred to this strange expedient of a marriage, instead of conquering the kingdom, and why Cleopatra bemeaned herself to marry the triumvir. The reply is not difficult to him who knows the history of Rome. There was a long-standing tradition in Roman policy to exploit Egypt but to respect its independence; it may be, because the country was considered more difficult to govern than in truth it was, or because there existed for this most ancient land, the seat of all the most refined arts, the most learned schools, the choicest industries, exceedingly rich and highly civilised, a regard that somewhat resembles what France imposes on the world to-day. Finally, it may be because it was held that if Egypt were annexed, its influence on Italy would be too much in the ascendent, and the traditions of the old Roman life would be conclusively overwhelmed by the invasion of the customs, the ideas, the refinements—in a word, by the corruptions of Egypt. Antony, who was set in the idea of repeating in Persia the adventure of Alexander the Great, did not dare bring about an annexation which would have been severely judged in Italy and which he, like the others, thought more dangerous than in reality it was. On the other hand, with a dynastic marriage, he was able to secure for himself all the advantages of effective possession, without running the risks of annexation; so he resolved upon this artifice, which, I repeat, had probably been imagined by Cæsar. As to Cleopatra, her government was menaced by a strong internal opposition, the causes for which are ill known; marrying Antony, she gathered about her throne, to protect it, formidable guards, the Roman legions.

To sum up, the romance of Antony and Cleopatra covers, at least in its beginnings, a political treaty. With the marriage, Cleopatra seeks to steady her wavering power; Antony, to place the valley of the Nile under the Roman protectorate. How then was the famous romance born? The actual history of Antony and Cleopatra is one of the most tragic episodes of a struggle that lacerated the Roman Empire for four centuries, until it finally destroyed it, the struggle between Orient and Occident. During the age of Cæsar, little by little, without any one's realising it at first, there arose and fulfilled itself a fact of the gravest importance; that is, the eastern part of the Empire had grown out of proportion: first, from the conquest of the Pontus, made by Lucullus, who had added immense territory in Asia Minor; then by Pompey's conquest of Syria, and the protectorate extended by him over all Palestine and a considerable part of Arabia. These new districts were not only enormous in extension; they were also populous, wealthy, fertile, celebrated for ancient culture; they held the busiest industrial cities, the best cultivated regions of the ancient world, the most famous seats of arts, letters, science, therefore their annexation, made rapidly in few years, could but trouble the already unstable equilibrium of the Empire. Italy was then, compared with these provinces, a poor and barbarous land; because southern Italy was ruined by the wars of preceding epochs, and northern Italy, naturally the wealthier part, was still crude and in the beginning of its development. The other western provinces nearer Italy were poorer and less civilised than Italy, except Gallia Narbonensis and certain parts of southern Spain. So that Rome, the capital of the Empire, came to find itself far from the richest and most populous regions, among territories poor and despoiled, on the frontiers of barbarism—in such a situation as the Russian Empire might find itself to-day if it had its capital at Vladivostok or Kharbin. You know that during the last years of the life of Cæsar it was rumoured several times that the Dictator wished to remove the capital of the Empire; it was said, to Alexandria in Egypt, to Ilium in the district where Troy arose. It is impossible to judge whether these reports were true or merely invented by enemies of Cæsar to damage him; at any rate, true or false, they show that public opinion was beginning to concern itself with the "Eastern peril"; that is, with the danger that the seat of empire must be shifted toward the Orient and the too ample Asiatic and African territory, and that Italy be one day uncrowned of her metropolitan predominance, conquered by so many wars. Such hear-says must have seemed, even if not true, the more likely, because, in his last two years, Cæsar planned the conquest of Persia. Now the natural basis of operations for the conquest of Persia was to be found, not in Italy, but in Asia Minor, and if Persia had been conquered, it would not have been possible to govern in Rome an empire so immeasurably enlarged in the Orient. Everything therefore induces to the belief that this question was at least discussed in the coterie of the friends of Cæsar; and it was a serious question, because in it the traditions, the aspirations, the interests of Italy were in irreconcilable conflict with a supreme necessity of state which one day or other would impose itself, if some unforeseen event did not intervene to solve it.

In the light of these considerations, the conduct of Antony becomes very clear. The marriage at Antioch, by which he places Egypt under the Roman protectorate, is the decisive act of a policy that looks to transporting the centre of his government toward the Orient, to be able to accomplish more securely the conquest of Persia. Antony, the heir of Cæsar, the man who held the papers of the Dictator, who knew his hidden thoughts, who wished to complete the plans cut off by his death, proposes to conquer Persia; to conquer Persia, he must rely on the Oriental provinces that were the natural basis of operations for the great enterprise; among these, Antony must support himself above all on Egypt, the richest and most civilised and most able to supply him with the necessary funds, of which he was quite in want. Therefore he married the Cleopatra whom, it was said at Rome, Cæsar himself had wished to marry — with whom, at any rate, Cæsar had much dallied and intrigued. Does not this juxtaposition of facts seem luminous to you? In 36 B.C., Antony marries Cleopatra, as a few years before he had married Octavia, the sister of the future Augustus, for political reasons — in order to be able to dispose of the political subsidies and finances of Egypt, for the conquest of Persia. The conquest of Persia is the ultimate motive of all his policy, the supreme explanation of his every act.

However, little by little, this move, made on both sides from considerations of political interest, altered its character under the action of events, of time, through the personal influence of Antony and Cleopatra upon each other, and above all, the power that Cleopatra acquired over Antony: here is truly the most important part of all this story. Those who have read my history know that I have recounted hardly any of the anecdotes, more or less odd or entertaining, with which ancient writers describe the intimate life of Antony and Cleopatra, because it is impossible to discriminate in them the part that is fact from that which was invented or exaggerated by political enmity. In history the difficulty of recognising the truth gradually increases as one passes from political to private life; because in politics the acts of men and of parties are always bound together by either causes or effects of which a certain number is always exactly known; private life, on the other hand, is, as it were, isolated and secret, almost invariably impenetrable. What a great man of state does in his own house, his valet knows better than the historians of later times.

If for these reasons I have thought it prudent not to accept in my work the stories and anecdotes that the ancients recount of Antony and Cleopatra, without indeed risking to declare them false, it is, on the contrary, not possible to deny that Cleopatra gradually acquired great ascendency over the mind of Antony. The circumstance is of itself highly probable. That Cleopatra was perhaps a Venus, as the ancients say, or that she was provided with but a mediocre beauty, as declare the portraits, matters little: it is, however, certain that she was a woman of great cleverness and culture; as woman and queen of the richest and most civilised realm of the ancient world, she was mistress of all those arts of pleasure, of luxury, of elegance, that are the most delicate and intoxicating fruit of all mature civilisations. Cleopatra might refigure, in the ancient world, the wealthiest, most elegant, and cultured Parisian lady in the world of to-day.

Antony, on the other hand, was the descendant of a family of that Roman nobility which still preserved much rustic roughness in tastes, ideas, habits; he grew up in times in which the children were still given Spartan training; he came to Egypt from a nation which, notwithstanding its military and diplomatic triumphs, could be considered, compared with Egypt, only poor, rude, and barbarous. Upon this intelligent man, eager for enjoyment, who had, like other noble Romans, already begun to taste the charms of intellectual civilisation, it was not Cleopatra alone that made the keenest of impressions, but all Egypt, the wonderful city of Alexandria, the sumptuous palace of the Ptolemies—all that refined, elegant splendour of which he found himself at one stroke the master. What was there at Rome to compare with Alexandria?—Rome, in spite of its imperial power, abandoned to a fearful disorder by the disregard of factions, encumbered with ruin, its streets narrow and wretched, provided as yet with but a single *forum,* narrow and plain, the sole impressive monument of which was the theatre of Pompey; Rome, where the life was yet crude, and objects of luxury so rare that they had to be brought from the distant Orient? At Alexandria, instead, the Paris of the ancient world, were to be found all the best and most beautiful things of the earth. There was a sumptuosity of public edifices that the ancients never tire of extolling—the quay seven *stadia* long, the light house famous all over the Mediterranean, the marvellous zoological garden, the Museum, the Gymnasium, innumerable temples, the unending palace of the Ptolemies. There was an abundance, unheard of for those times, of objects of luxury—rugs, glass, stuffs, papyruses, jewels, artistic pottery—because they made all these things at Alexandria. There was an abundance, greater than elsewhere, of silk, of perfumes, of gems, of all the things imported from the extreme East, because through Alexandria passed one of the most frequented routes of Indo-Chinese commerce. There, too, were innumerable artists, writers, philosophers, and *savants;* society life and intellectual life alike fervid; continuous movement to and fro of traffic, continual passing of rare and curious things; countless amusements; life, more than elsewhere, safe—at least so it was believed—because at Alexandria were the great schools of medicine and the great scientific physicians.

If other Italians who landed in Alexandria were dazzled by so many splendours, Antony ought to have been blinded; *he* entered Alexandria as King. He who was born at Rome in the small and simple house of an impoverished noble family, who had been brought up with Latin parsimony to eat frugally, to drink wine only on festival occasions, to wear the same clothes a long time, to be served by a single slave—this man found himself lord of the immense palace of the Ptolemies, where the kitchens alone were a hundred times larger than the house of his fathers at Rome; where there were gathered for his pleasure the most precious treasures and the most marvellous collections of works of art; where there were trains of servants at his command, and every wish could be immediately gratified. It is therefore not necessary to suppose that Antony was foolishly enamoured of the Queen of Egypt, to understand the change that took place in him after their marriage, as he tasted the inimitable life of Alexandria, that elegance, that ease, that wealth, that pomp without equal.

A man of action, grown in simplicity, toughened by a rude life, he was all at once carried into the midst of the subtlest and most highly developed civilisation of the ancient world and given the greatest facilities to enjoy and abuse it that ever man had: as might have been expected, he was intoxicated; he contracted an almost insane passion for such a life; he adored Egypt with such ardour as to forget for it the nation of his birth and the modest home of his boyhood. And then began the great tragedy of his life, a tragedy not love-inspired, but political. As the hold of Egypt strengthened on his mind, Cleopatra tried to persuade him not to conquer Persia, but to accept openly the kingdom of Egypt, to found with her and with their children a new dynasty, and to create a great new Egyptian Empire, adding to Egypt the better part of the provinces that Rome possessed in Africa and in Asia, abandoning Italy and the provinces of the West forever to their destiny.

Cleopatra had thought to snatch from Rome its Oriental Empire by the arm of Antony, in that immense disorder of revolution; to reconstruct the great Empire of Egypt, placing at its head the first general of the time, creating an army of Roman legionaries with the gold of the Ptolemies; to make Egypt and its dynasty the prime potentate of Africa and Asia, transferring to Alexandria the political and diplomatic control of the finest parts of the Mediterranean world.

As the move failed, men have deemed it folly and stupidity; but he who knows how easy it is to be wise after events, will judge this confused policy of Cleopatra less curtly. At any rate, it is certain that her scheme failed more because of its own inconsistencies than through the vigour and ability with which Rome tried to thwart it; it is certain that in the execution of the plan, Antony felt first in himself the tragic discord between Orient and Occident that was so long to lacerate the Empire; and of that tragic discord he was the first victim. An enthusiastic admirer of Egypt, an ardent Hellenist, he is lured by his great ambition to be king of Egypt, to renew the famous line of the Ptolemies, to continue in the East the glory and the traditions of Alexander the Great: but the far-away voice of his fatherland still sounds in his ear; he recalls the city of his birth, the Senate in which he rose so many times to speak, the *Forum* of his orations, the Comitia that elected him to magistracies; Octavia, the gentlewoman he had wedded with the sacred rites of Latin monogamy; the friends and soldiers with whom he had fought through so many countries in so many wars; the foundation principles at home that ruled the family, the state, morality, public and private.

Cleopatra's scheme, viewed from Alexandria, was an heroic undertaking, almost divine, that might have lifted him and his scions to the delights of Olympus; seen from Rome, by his childhood's friends, by his comrades in arms, by that people of Italy who still so much admired him, it was the shocking crime of faithlessness to his country; we call it high treason. Therefore he hesitates long, doubting most of all whether he can keep for the new Egyptian Empire the Roman legions, made up largely of Italians, all commanded by

Italian officers. He does not know how to oppose a resolute *No* to the insistences of Cleopatra and loose himself from the fatal bond that keeps him near her; he can not go back to live in Italy after having dwelt as king in Alexandria. Moreover, he does not dare declare his intentions to his Roman friends, fearing they will scatter; to the soldiers, fearing they will revolt; to Italy, fearing her judgment of him as a traitor; and so, little by little, he entangles himself in the crooked policy, full of prevarications, of expedients, of subterfuges, of one mistake upon another, that leads him to Actium.

I think I have shown that Antony succumbed in the famous war not because, mad with love, he abandoned the command in the midst of the battle, but because his armies revolted and abandoned him when they understood what he had not dared declare to them openly: that he meant to dismember the Empire of Rome to create the new Empire of Alexandria. The future Augustus conquered at Actium without effort, merely because the national sentiment of the soldiery, outraged by the unforeseen revelation of Antony's treason, turned against the man who wanted to aggrandise Cleopatra at the expense of his own country.

And then the victorious party, the party of Augustus, created the story of Antony and Cleopatra that has so entertained posterity; this story is but a popular explanation—in part imaginatively exaggerated and fantastic—of the Eastern peril that menaced Rome, of both its political phase and its moral. According to the story that Horace has put into such charming verse, Cleopatra wished to conquer Italy, to enslave Rome, to destroy the Capitol; but Cleopatra alone could not have accomplished so difficult a task; she must have seduced Antony, made him forget his duty to his wife, to his legitimate children, to the Republic, the soldiery, his native land,—all the duties that Latin morals inculcated into the minds of the great, and that a shameless Egyptian woman, rendered perverse by all the arts of the Orient, had blotted out in his soul; therefore Antony's tragic fate should serve as a solemn warning to distrust the voluptuous seductions, of which Cleopatra symbolised the elegant and fatal depravity. The story was magnified, coloured, diffused, not because it was beautiful and romantic, but because it served the interests of the political *coterie* that gained definite control of the government on the ruin of Antony. At Actium, the future Augustus did not fight a real war, he only passively watched the power of the adversary go to pieces, destroyed by its own internal contradictions. He did not decide to conquer Egypt until the public opinion of Italy, enraged against Antony and Cleopatra, required this vengeance with such insistence that he had to satisfy it.

If Augustus was not a man too quick in action, he was, instead, keenly intelligent in comprehending the situation created by the catastrophe of Antony in Italy, where already, for a decade of years, public spirit, frightened by revolution, was anxious to return to the ways of the past, to the historic sources of the national life. Augustus understood that he ought to stand before Italy, disgusted as it was with long-continued dissension and eager to retrace the way of national tradition, as the embodiment of all the virtues his contemporaries set in opposition to eastern "corruption,"—simplicity, severity of private habits, rigid monogamy, the antifeministic spirit, the purely virile idea of the state. Naturally, the exaltation of these virtues required the portrayal in his rival of Actium, as far as possible, the opposite defects; therefore the efforts of his friends, like Horace, to colour the story of Antony and Cleopatra, which should magnify to the Italians the idea of the danger from which Augustus had saved them at Actium; which was meant to serve as a barrier against the invading Oriental "corruption," that "corruption" the essence of which I have already analysed.

In a certain sense, the legend of Antony and Cleopatra is chiefly an antifeminist legend, intended to reinforce in the state the power of the masculine principle, to demonstrate how dangerous it may be to leave to women the government of public affairs, or follow their counsel in political business.

The people believed the legend; posterity has believed it. Two years ago when I published in the *Revue de Paris* an article in which I demonstrated, by obvious arguments, the incongruities and absurdities of the legend, and tried to retrace through it the half-effaced lines of the truth, everybody was amazed. From one end of Europe to the other, the papers resuméd the conclusions of my study as an astounding revelation. An illustrious French statesman, a man of the finest culture in historical study, Joseph Reinach, said to me:

> After your article I have re-read Dion and Plutarch. It is indeed singular that for twenty centuries men have read and re-read those pages without any one's realising how confused and absurd their accounts are.

It seems to be a law of human psychology that almost all historic personages, from Minos to Mazzini, from Judas to Charlotte Corday, from Xerxes to Napoleon, are imaginary personages; some transfigured into demigods, by admiration and success; the others debased by hate and failure. In reality, the former were often uglier, the latter more attractive than tradition has pictured them, because men in general are neither too good nor too bad, neither too intelligent nor too stupid. In conclusion, historic tradition is full of deformed caricatures and ideal transfigurations; because, when they are dead, the impression of their political contemporaries still serves the ends of parties, states, nations, institutions. Can this man exalt in a people the consciousness of its own power, of its own energy, of its own value? Lo, then they make a god of him, as of Napoleon or Bismarck. Can this other serve to feed in the mass, odium and scorn of another party, of a government, of an order of things that it is desirable to injure? Then they make a monster of him, as happened in Rome to Tiberius, in France to Napoleon III, in Italy to all who for one motive or another opposed the unification of Italy.

It is true that after a time the interests that have coloured certain figures with certain hues and shades disappear; but then the reputation, good or bad, of a personage is already made; his name is stamped on the memory of posterity with an adjective,—the great, the wise, the wicked, the cruel, the rapacious,—and there is no human force that can dissever name from adjective. Some faraway historian, studying all the documents, examining the sequence of events, will confute the tradition in learned books; but his work not only will not succeed in persuading the ignorant multitude, but must also contend against the multiplied objections offered by the instinctive incredulity of people of culture.

You will say to me, "What is the use of writing history? Why spend so much effort to correct the errors in which people will persist just as if the histories were never written?" I reply that I do not believe that the office of history is to give to men who have guided the great human events a posthumous justice. It is already work serious enough for every generation to give a little justice to the living, rather than occupy itself rendering it to the dead, who indeed, in contradistinction from the living, have no need of it. The study of history, the rectification of stories of the past, ought to serve another and practical end; that is, train the men who govern nations to discern more clearly than may be possible from their own environment the truth underlying the legends. As I have already said, passions, interests, present historic personages in a thousand forms when they are alive, transfiguring not only the persons themselves, but events the most diverse, the character of institutions, the conditions of nations.

It is generally believed that legends are found only at the dawn of history, in the poetic period: that is a great mistake; the legend—the legend that deceives, that deforms, that misdirects—is everywhere, in all ages, in the present as in the past—in the present even more than in the past, because it is the consequence of certain universal forms of thought and of sentiment. To-day, just as ten or twenty centuries ago, interests and passions dominate events, alter them and distort them, creating about them veritable romances, more or less probable. The present, which appears to all to be the same reality, is instead, for most people, only a huge legend, traversed by contemporaries stirred by the most widely differing sentiments.

However the mass may content itself with this legend, throbbing with hate and love, with hope and the fear of its own self-created phantoms, those who guide and govern the masses ought to try to divine the truth, as far as they can. A great man of state is distinguished from a mediocre by his greater ability to divine the real in his world of action beneath its superfice of confused legends; by his greater ability to discriminate in everything what is true from what is merely apparently true, in the prestige of states and institutions, in the forces of parties, in the energy attributed to certain men, in the purposes claimed by parties and men, often different from their real designs. To do that, some natural disposition is necessary, a liveliness of intuition that must come with birth; but this faculty can be refined and trained by a practical knowledge of men, by experience in things, and by the study of history. In the ages dead, when the interests that created their legends have disappeared, we can discover how those great popular delusions, which are one of the greatest forces of history, are made and how they work. We may thus fortify the spirit to withstand the cheating illusions that surround us, coming from every part of the vast modern world, in which so many interests dispute dominion over thoughts and will.

In this sense alone, I believe that history may teach, not the multitude, which will never learn anything from it, but, impelled by the same passions, will always repeat the same errors and the same foolishnesses; but the chosen few, who, charged with directing the game of history, have concern in knowing as well as they can its inner law. Taken in this way, history may be a great teacher, in its every page, every line, and the study of the legend of Antony and Cleopatra may itself even serve to prepare the spirit of a diplomat, who must treat between state and state the complicated economic and political affairs of the modern world. And so, in conclusion, history and life interchange mutual services; life teaches history, and history, life; observing the present, we help ourselves to know the past, and from the study of the past we can return to our present the better tempered and prepared to observe and comprehend it. In present and in past, history can form a kind of wisdom set apart, in a certain sense aristocratic, above what the masses know, at least as to the universal laws that govern the life of nations.

THE DEVELOPMENT OF GAUL

IN estimating distant historical events, one is often the victim of an error of perspective; that is, one is disposed to consider as the outcome of a pre-established plan of human wisdom what is the final result, quite unforeseen, of causes that acted beyond the foresight of contemporaries. At the distance of centuries, turning back to consider the past, we can easily find out that the efforts of one or two generations have produced certain effects on the actual condition of the world; and then we conclude that those generations meant to reach that result. On the contrary, men almost always face the future proposing to themselves impossible ends; notwithstanding which, their efforts, accumulating, destroying, interweaving, bring into being consequences that no one had foreseen or planned, the novelty or importance of which often only future generations realise. Columbus, who, fixed in the idea of reaching India by sailing west, finds America on his way and does not recognise it at once but is persuaded that he has landed in India, symbolises the lot of man in history.

Of this phenomenon, which is to me a fundamental law of history, there is a classic example in the story of Rome: the conquest of Gaul. Without doubt, one of the greatest works of Rome was the conquest and Romanisation of Gaul: indeed that conquest and Romanisation of Gaul is the beginning of European civilisation; for before the Græco-Latin civilisation reached the Rhine over the ways opened by the Roman sword, the continent of Europe had centres of civilisation on the coast or in its projecting extremities, like Italy, Bætica, Narbonensis; but the interior was still entirely in the power of a turbulent and restless barbarism, like the African continent to-day. Moreover, what Rome created in Asia and Africa was almost entirely destroyed by ages following; on the contrary, Rome yet lives in France, to which it gave its language, its spirit, and the traditions of its thought. Exactly for this reason it is particularly important to explain how such an outcome was brought about, and by what historic forces. From the propensity to consider every great historical event as wholly a masterpiece of human genius, many historians have attributed also this accomplishment to a prodigious, well-nigh divine wisdom on the part of the Romans, and Julius Cæsar is regarded as a demigod who had fixed his gaze upon the far, far distant future. However, it is not difficult, studying the ancient documents with critical spirit, to persuade oneself that even if Cæsar was a man of genius, he was not a god; that from beginning to end, the real story of the conquest of Gaul is very different from the commonly accepted version.

I hope to demonstrate that Cæsar threw himself into the midst of Gallic affairs, impelled by slight incidents of internal politics, not only without giving any thought whatever to the future destiny of Gaul, but without even knowing well the conditions existing there. Gaul was then for all Romans a barbarous region, poor, gloomy, full of swamps and forests in which there would be much fighting and little booty: no one was thinking then of having Roman territory cross the Alps; everyone was infatuated by the story of Alexander the Great, dreaming only of conquering like him all the rich and civilised Orient; everyone, even Cæsar. Only a sequence of political accidents pushed him in spite of himself into Gaul.

In 62 B.C., Pompey had returned from the Orient, where he had finished the conquest of Pontus, begun by Lucullus, and annexed Syria. On his return, the conservative party, irritated against him because he had gone over to the opposite side, and having been given something to think of by the prestige that the policy of expansion was winning for the popular party, had succeeded by many intrigues in keeping the Senate from ratifying what he had done in the East. This internal struggle closed the Orient for several years to the adventurous initiatives of the political imperialists; for as long as the adminstration of Pompey remained unapproved, it was impossible to think of undertaking new enterprises or conquests in Asia and Africa; and therefore, of necessity, Roman politics, burning for conquest and adventure, had to turn to another part of Europe.

The letters of Cicero prove to us that Cæsar was not the first to think that Rome, having its hands tied for the moment in the East, ought to interfere in the affairs of Gaul. The man who first had the idea of a Gallic policy was Quintus Metellus Celerus, husband of the famous Clodia, and consul the year before Cæsar. Taking advantage of certain disturbances arisen in Gaul from the constant wars between the differing parts, Metellus had persuaded the Senate to authorise him to make war on the Helvetians. At the beginning of the year 59, that is, the year in which Cæsar was consul, Metellus was already preparing to depart for the war in Gaul, when suddenly he died; and then Cæsar, profiting by the interest in Rome for Gallic affairs, had the mission previously entrusted to Metellus given to himself and took up both Metellus's office and his plan. Here you see at the beginning of this story the first accident,—the death of Metellus. An historian curious of nice and unanswerable questions might ask himself what would have been the history of the world if Metellus had not died. Certainly Rome would have been occupied with Gallic concerns a year sooner and by a different man; Cæsar would probably have had to seek elsewhere a brilliant proconsulship and things Gallic would have for ever escaped his energy.

However it be, charged with the affairs of Gaul accidentally and unexpectedly, Cæsar went there without well knowing the condition of it, and, in fact, as I think I proved in a long appendix published in the French and English editions of my work, he began his Gallic policy with a serious mistake; that is, attacking the Helvetians. A superior mind, Cæsar was not long in finding his bearings in the midst of the tremendous confusion he found in Gaul; but for this, there is no need to think that he carried out in the Gallic policy vast schemes, long meditated: he worked, instead, as the uncertain changes of Roman politics imposed. I believe that there is but one way to understand and reasonably explain the policy pursued by Cæsar in Gaul, his sudden moves, his zigzags, his audacities, his mistakes; that is, to study it from Rome, to keep always in mind the internal changes, the party struggle, in which he was involved at Rome. In short, Gaul was for Cæsar only a means to operate on the internal politics of Rome, of which he made use from day to day, as the immediate interest of the passing hour seemed to require.

I cite a single example, but the most significant. Cæsar declared Gaul a Roman province and annexed it to the Empire toward the end of 57 B.C.; that is, at the end of his second year as proconsul, unexpectedly, with no warning act to intimate such vigorous intent, —a surprise; and why? Look to Rome and you will understand. In 57 B.C., the democratic party, demoralised by discords, upset by the popular agitation to recall Cicero from unjust exile, discredited by scandals, especially the Egyptian scandals, seemed on the point of going to pieces. Cæsar understood that there was but one way to stop this ruin: to stun public opinion and all Italy with some highly audacious surprise. The surprise was the annexation of Gaul. Declaring Gaul a Roman province after the victory over the Belgi, he convinced Rome that he had in two years overcome all Gallic adversaries. And so, the conquest of Gaul—this event that was to open a new era, this event, the effects of which still endure—was, at the beginning in the mind that conceived and executed it, nothing but a bold political expedient in behalf of a party, to solve a situation compromised by manifold errors.

But you will ask me: how from so tiny a seed could ever grow so mighty a tree, covering with its branches so much of the earth? You know that at the close of the proconsulship in Gaul, there breaks out a great civil war; this lasts, with brief interruptions and pauses, until the battle of Actium. Only toward 30 B.C., is the tempest lulled, and during this time Gaul seems almost to disappear; the ancient writers hardly mention it, except from time to time for a moment to let us know that some unimportant revolt broke out, now here, now there, in the vast territory; that this or that general was sent to repress it.

The civil wars ended, the government of Rome turns its attention to the provinces anew, but for another reason. Saint Jerome tells us that in 25 B.C., Augustus increased the tribute from the Gauls: we find no difficulty in getting at the reason of this fact. The thing most urgent after the re-establishment of peace was the re-arrangement of finance; that signified then, as always, an increase of imposts: but more could not be extorted from the Oriental provinces, already exhausted by so many wars and plunderings; therefore the idea to draw greater revenues from the European provinces of recent conquest, particularly from Gaul, which until then had paid so little. So you see a-forging one link after another in the chain: Cæsar for a political interest conquers Gaul; thirty years afterward Augustus goes there to seek new revenues for his balance-sheet; thenceforward there are always immediate needs that urge Roman politics into Gallic affairs: and so it is that little by little Roman politics become permanently involved, by a kind of concatenation, not by deliberate plan.

We can easily follow the process. Augustus had left in Gaul to exact the new tribute, a former slave of Cæsar's, afterward liberated, —a Gaul or German whom Cæsar had captured as a child in one of his expeditions and later freed, because of his consummate administrative ability. It appears, however, that, for the Gauls at least, this ability was even too great. In a curious chapter Dion tells us that Licinius, this freedman, uniting the avarice of a barbarian to the pretences of a Roman, beat down everyone that seemed greater than he; oppressed all those who seemed to have more power; extorted enormous sums from all, were they to fill out the dues of his office, or to enrich himself and his family. His rascality was so stupendous that since the Gauls paid certain taxes every month, he increased to fourteen the number of the months, declaring that December, the last, was only the tenth; consequently it was necessary to count two more, one called Undecember and another, Duodecember.

I would not guarantee this story true, since, when there is introduced into a nation a new and more burdensome system of taxes, there are always set in circulation tales of this kind about the rapacity of the persons charged with collecting them: but true or false, the tale shows that the Gauls were much irritated by the new tribute; indeed this irritation increased so much that in the winter from the year 15 till the year 14 B.C., Augustus, having to remain in Gaul on account of certain serious complications, arisen in Germany, was obliged to give his attention to it during his stay. The prominent men of Gaul presented vigorous complaints to him against Licinius and his administration. Then there occurred an episode that, recounted three centuries later with a certain naïveté by Dion Cassius, has been overlooked by the historians, but which seems to me to be of prime interest in the history of the Latin world. Dion writes:

> Augustus, not able to avoid blaming Licinius for the many denunciations and revelations of the Gallic chiefs, sought in other things to excuse him; he pretended not to know certain facts, made believe not to accept others, being ashamed to have placed such a procurator in Gaul. Licinius, however, extricated himself from the danger by a decidedly original expedient. When he realised that Augustus was displeased and that he was running great risk of being punished, he conducted that Prince to his house, and showing him his numerous treasuries full of gold and silver, enormous piles of objects made of precious metals, said: — "My lord, only for your good and that of the Romans have I amassed all these riches. I feared that the natives, fortified by such wealth, might revolt, if I left them to them: therefore I have placed them in safe-keeping for you and I give them to you." So, by his pretext that he had thus broken the power of the barbarians for the sake of Augustus, Licinius saved himself from danger.

This incident has without doubt the smack of legend. Ought we therefore to conclude that it is wholly invented? No, because in history the distortions of the truth are much more numerous than are inventions. This page of Dion is important. It preserves for us, presented in a dramatic scene between Augustus and Licinius, the record of a very serious dispute carried on between the notable men of Gaul and Licinius, in the presence of Augustus. The Gauls complain of paying too many imposts: Licinius replies that Gaul is very rich; that it grows rich quickly and therefore it ought to pay as much as is demanded of it, and more. Not only did the freedman show rooms full of gold and silver to his lord; he showed him the great economic progress of Gaul, its marvellous future, the immense wealth concealed in its soil and in the genius of its inhabitants. In other words, this chapter of Dion makes us conclude that Rome— that is, the small oligarchy that was directing its politics—realised that the Gaul conquered by Cæsar, the Gaul that had always been considered as a country cold and sterile, was instead a magnificent province, naturally rich, from which they might get enormous treasure. This discovery was made in the winter of 15–14 B.C.; that is, forty-three years after Cæsar had added the province to the Empire; forty-three years after they had possessed without knowing what they possessed, like some *grand seigneur* who unwittingly holds among the common things of his patrimony some priceless object, the value of which only an accident on a sudden reveals.

This chapter of Dion allows us also to affirm that he who first realised the value of Gaul and opened the eyes of Augustus, was no great personage of the Roman aristocracy whose names are written in such lofty characters on the pages of history, whose images are yet found in marble and bronze among the museums of Europe; no one of those who ruled the Empire and therefore according to reason and justice had the responsibility of governing it well: it was, instead, an obscure freedman, whose ability the masters of the Empire scorned to exploit except as to-day a peasant uses the forces of his ox, hardly deigning to look at him and yet deeming all his labour but the owner's natural right.

So stands the story. The Gallic freedman observed, and understood, and was forgotten; posterity, instead, has had to wonder over the profound wisdom of the Roman aristocrat, who understood nothing. Moreover, if in 14 B.C. Licinius had to make an effort to persuade the surprised and diffident Augustus that Gaul was a province of great future, it is clear that Gaul must already have begun to grow rich by itself without the Roman government's having done anything to promote its progress.

From what hidden sources sprang forth this new wealth of Gaul? All the documents that we possess authorise us to respond that Gaul — to begin from the time of Augustus — was able to grow rich quickly, because the events following the Roman conquest turned and disposed the general conditions of the Empire in its favour. Gaul then, as France now, was endowed with several requisites essential to its becoming a nation of great economic development: a land very fertile; a population dense for the times, intelligent, wide-awake, active; a climate that, even though it seemed to Greeks and Romans cold and foggy, was better suited to intense activity than the warm and sunny climate of the South; and finally, — a supreme advantage in ancient civilisation, — it was everywhere intersected, as by a network of canals, by navigable rivers. In ancient times transport by land was very expensive; water was the natural and economic vehicle of commerce; therefore civilisation was able to enter with commerce into the interior of continents only by way of the rivers, which, as one might say, were to a certain extent the railroads of the ancient world.

To these advantageous conditions, which, being physical, existed before the Roman conquest, the conquest added some others: it broke down the political barrier that previously cut off these convenient means of penetration, the rivers; it suppressed the wars between the Gallic tribes, the privileges, the tyrannies, the tolls, the monopolies; it saved the enormous resources that were previously wasted in these constant drains; it put again the hoe, the spade, the tools of the artisan, into hands that had before been wielding the sword; and finally, it consolidated (and this was perhaps the most important effect) the jurisdiction of property. When Cæsar invaded Gaul, the great landowners still cultivated cereals and textile plants but little; they put the greater part of their fortune into cattle, exactly because in that régime of continual war and revolution lands easily kept changing proprietors. Futhermore, the more frequent contact with Rome acquainted the Gauls with Roman agriculture and its abler methods, with Latin life and its studied order.

By the combination of all these causes, population and production increased rapidly. The gain in population was so considerable that the ancients themselves noticed it. Strabo (Bk. 4, ch. i, §2) observes that the Gallic women are fecund mothers and excellent nurses. With the population, wealth increased on all sides, in agriculture as in industry and in trade.

The new and more stable jurisdiction of the landed proprietary generated another most important effect; it promoted rapidly the cultivation of cereals and textile plants, of wheat and flax. "All Gaul produces much wheat," says Strabo, and we read his notice without surprise, because we know that France is, even to-day, the region of Europe most fertile in cereals. There is no reason to suppose that it must have been barren of them twenty centuries ago. Other documentary evidence, particularly inscriptions, confirms Strabo, informing us that, especially in the second century, Rome bought the customary grain to feed the metropolis not only in Egypt, but also in Gaul. In short, Gaul seems to have been the sole region of Europe fertile enough to be able to export grain, to have been for Rome a kind of Canada or Middle West of the time, set not beyond oceans but beyond the Alps.

The cultivation of flax, to the ancient world what cotton is to-day, progressed rapidly in Gaul along with that of wheat, so that Gaul was early able to rival Egypt also in this respect. That Gaul and Egypt should have so much in common at the same time, was something so interesting and seemed so strange that Pliny himself wrote:

Flax is sowed only in sandy places and after a single ploughing. Perhaps Egypt may be pardoned for sowing it, because with it she buys the merchandise of India and Arabia. But, look you!—even Gaul is famous for this plant. What matters it, if huge mountains shut away the sea; if on the ocean side it has for confines what is called emptiness? Notwithstanding that, Gaul cultivates flax like Egypt: the Cadurci, the Caleti, the Ruteni, the Biturigi, the Morini, who are considered tribes of the ends of the earth . . . but what am I saying? All Gaul makes sails,—till the enemies beyond the Rhine imitate them, and the linen is more beautiful to the eyes than are their women.

These descriptions show Gaul to be one of the new countries, like the Argentine Republic or the United States, in which the land has still almost its natural pristine fecundity and brings forth a marvellous abundance of plants that clothe and nourish man. We know that in Gaul under the Empire there were immense fortunes in land in face of which the fortunes of wealthy Italian proprietors shrink like the fortunes of Europe when compared with the great ranch fortunes of the Argentine Republic or the United States. Twenty years ago they began to excavate in France the ruins of the great Gallo-Roman villas: these are constructed on the plan of the Italian villa, decorated in the same way, but are much larger, more sumptuous, more sightly; one feels in them the pride of a new people which has adopted the Latin civilisation, but has infused into that, derived from the wealth of their land, a spirit of grandeur and of luxury that poorer and older Latins did not know, exactly as to-day the Americans infuse a spirit of greater magnitude and boldness into so many things that they take from timid, old Europe. Perhaps there was also in this Gallic luxury, as in the American, a bit of ostentation, intended to humiliate the masters remaining poorer and more modest.

But Gaul was a nation not only rich in fertilest agriculture; side by side with that, progressed its industry. This, according to my notion, is one of the vital points in ancient history. Under the

Roman domination, Gaul was not restricted to the better cultivation of its productive soil; but alone among the peoples of the Occident, became, as we might now say, an industrial nation, that manufactured not only by and for itself, but like Asia Minor, Egypt, Syria, sold also to other peoples of the Empire and outside of its own boundaries; in a word, exported. The more frequent contact with the Orient better acquainted the Gauls with the beautiful objects made by the artisans of Laodicea, of Tyre, of Sidon; and the clever genius of the Celt, always apt in industry, drew from them incentive to create a Gallic industry, partly imitative, partly original, and to seek a large *clientèle* for these industries in Italy, in Spain, beyond the Rhine, among the Germans, in the Danube provinces. This is proved by a number of important passages in Pliny, confirmed by inscriptions and archæological discoveries.

Pliny has already told us that the Gauls manufactured many linen sails; we know also that they made not only rough sails, but also fine linen for clothing, which had a wide market. There have been found in the Orient numerous fragments of an inscription containing the famous edict of Diocletian on maximum sale prices allowed, an inscription of value to us for its nomenclature of ancient fabrics. In this nomenclature is mentioned the *birrus* of Laodicea, an imitation of the *birrus* of the Nervii, which was a very fine linen cloth, worn by ladies of fashion. Laodicea was one of the most ancient centres of Oriental textile fabrics; the Nervii were one of the most remote of the Gallic peoples, living—the coincidence is noteworthy—about where Flanders is now. If at Laodicea they made at the end of the third century an imitation of Nervian linen, that means that the Nervii had succeeded in manufacturing and finding market for cloth so desirable as to rouse the Laodiceans, competing for trade, to imitate it. What proof more persuasive that during the early centuries of the Empire the Gauls greatly improved their industries and widened their markets?

They had mastered weaving, but they did not stop there; they invented new methods of dyeing, using vegetable dyes instead of the customary animal colours of the Orient. Pliny says:

The Gaul imitates with herbs all colours, including Tyrian purple; they do not seek the mollusk on the sea bottom; they run no risk of being devoured by sea monsters; they do not exploit the anchorless deep to multiply the attractions of the courtesan, or to increase the powers of the seducer of another's wife. They gather the herbs like cereals, standing on the dry ground; although the colour that they derive does not bear washing. Luxury could thus be gratified with greater show at the cost of fewer dangers.

It is clear, then, according to Pliny, at one time, it was believed that the competition of Gallic dyers might have ruined the Oriental, and would have done so, had the tenacity of their vegetable colouring equalled its beauty. In another passage Pliny tells us that these Gallic stuffs were used especially by the slaves and the populace.

The wool industry made no less progress in Gaul than weaving and dyeing. From numerous passages in Juvenal and Martial it appears that the woollen clothing worn by the populace of Rome in the second century was woven in Gaul, particularly in the districts to-day known as Arras, Langres, Saintonge. Pliny attributes to the Gauls the invention of a wool, that, soaked in acid, became incombustible, and was used to make mattresses.

Glass-making was another art carried from the East across the Mediterranean into Gaul. Still another industry, metallurgy, after weaving, contributed greatly to enrich Gaul. Undoubtedly even before the Roman conquest, Gaul worked gold mines; it seems, however, that silver mines remained untouched until about the time of Augustus. At any rate, the discovery of some deposits of gold and silver then gave a spur to several flourishing industries; jewelry-making, and—an original Gallic industry of much importance—silver-plating and tinning. Here is another extract from Pliny, from which you will see that in those times they already made in France "Christofle" silver-plate:

They cover [writes Pliny] the copper with tin in such a way that it is difficult to distinguish it from silver. It is a Gallic invention. Later they began to do the same thing with silver, silver-plating especially the ornaments of horses and carriages. The merit of the invention belongs to the Biturigi, and the industry was developed in the city of Alesia. After the same fashion there has been spread everywhere a foolish profusion of objects not only silver-, but gold-plated. All that is called *cultus,* elegance!

We might almost say that Gallic industry did to the old industries of the ancient world what German wares have done compared with older and more aristocratic products of France, of England, popularising objects of luxury for the many and the merely well-to-do.

Finally, if any one hesitated to trust fully these very important passages in Pliny, he would be quite convinced by reading the great work of Dechelette. This author, studying with Carthusian patience and the ablest critical acumen the Gallic ceramics to be found scattered among the museums, has demonstrated most commendably that in the first century of the Empire many manufactories of ceramics were opened and flourished in Gaul, especially in the valley of the Allier, and that they sold their vases in Spain, in the Danube regions, to the Germans, and in Italy.

Dechelette has proved that many ceramics found among the ruins of Pompeii, now admired in the museums of Pompeii and Naples, were made in Gaul, — discoveries most noteworthy, which, in connection with the extracts from Pliny, disclose in essence that real Roman Gaul whose sumptuous relics but half tell the tale of its wealth.

This tremendous development of Gaul was without doubt an effect of the Roman conquest; but an effect that neither Cæsar, nor any other man of his times had foreseen or willed, but which Augustus was first to recognise in the winter of 15–14 B.C., and to which, astute man that he was, he gave heed as he ought; that is, not as due his own merit, but as an unexpected piece of good fortune. I have already said that one of the greatest cares of Augustus, as soon as the civil wars were finished, was to reorganise the finances of the Empire; that to find new entries for the treasury, he had turned his attention in 27 B.C. to the province conquered by his father, regarding it merely from the common point of view, as poor and of little worth like the other European territories. Then, at a stroke, he realised that that territory so lightly valued, was producing grain like Egypt, linen like Egypt; that the arts of civilisation for which Egypt was so rich and famous were beginning to prosper there! Augustus was not the man to let slip so tremendous a piece of good luck. Until then he had hesitated, like one who seeks his way; in that winter from 15–14 B.C., he found finally the grand climax of his career, to make Gaul the Egypt of the West, the province of the greatest revenues in Europe. From that time on to the end of his life, he did not move from Europe; he lived between Italy and Gaul. Like him, Tiberius, Drusus, all the men of his family, devoted all their efforts to Gaul, to consolidating Roman dominion there, to advancing its progress, to increasing the revenues, to making it actually the Occidental Egypt. From Velleius we learn that under Tiberius Gaul rendered to the Empire as much as did Egypt, and that Gaul and Egypt were considered alike the two richest imperial provinces.

As a political interest had at first impelled Cæsar to annex Gaul, an immediate financial interest urged Augustus to continue the work, to take care of the new province. Then the historic law that I have already enunciated to you, the law by which the efforts of men result far differently from that which they had intended, was verified anew by Augustus also, and in a new form. He had created his Gallic policy to augment the revenues of the Empire; the consequences of this fiscal policy, necessity-inspired, were greater than he and his friends ever dreamed. The winter of 15–14 B.C. is a notable date in the story of Latin civilisation, for then the destiny of the Empire was irrevocably settled; the Roman Empire will be made up of two parts, the Oriental and the Occidental, each part sufficiently strong to withstand being overcome by the other; it will be neither an Asiatic, nor a Celtic-Latin, but a mixed Empire: between both parts, Italy will rule for two centuries more, and Rome, an immense city, at once Oriental and Latin, will keep the metropolitan crown won from the enfeebled East, and dominate the immature barbarian West.

Speaking of Cleopatra, I have shown you how great was the Oriental peril that threatened in the last century of the Republic to wipe out Rome. What miraculous force saved it? Gaul. Suppose that the army of Cæsar had been exterminated at Alesia; suppose that Rome, discouraged, had abandoned its Gallic enterprise as it had done with Persia, after the disaster of Crassus and the failure of Antony; or suppose that Gaul had been a poor province, sterile and unpopulous, like many a Danube district; Rome could not have held out long as the seat of imperial government, just as to-day the capital of the Russian Empire could not maintain itself at Vladivostok or Harbin. It would have been necessary to move the metropolis to a richer and more populous region. That Gaul grew rich and was Romanised, changed the state of things. When Rome possessed beyond the Alps in Europe a province as large and as full of resources as Egypt; when there was the same interest in defending it as in defending Egypt, Italy was well placed to govern both. The Egypt of the Occident counterbalanced the Egypt of the Orient, and Rome, half way between, was the natural and necessary metropolis of the widespread Empire. Gaul alone, revived, so to speak, the Empire in the West and prevented the European provinces — even Italy itself — from becoming dead limbs safely amputable from the Oriental body. Gaul upheld Italy and Rome in Europe for three centuries longer; Gaul stopped it on the way to the Asiatic conquests run through by Alexander. Had it not been for Gaul, Asia Minor, Syria, and Egypt would have formed the real Empire of Rome, and Italy would have been lost in it: without Gaul, the

Orientalised Empire would have tried to conquer Persia and probably succeeded in doing so, abandoning the poor and unproductive lands of the untamed Occident. In short, Gaul created in the Roman Empire that duality between East and West which gives shape to all the history of our civilisation; it kept the artificial form of the Empire, circular about an island sea; it inspired the Empire with that double self-contradictory spirit, Latin and Oriental, at once its strength and its weakness.

Next time I will show you the continuation of this struggle of two minds, in a characteristic episode, the story of the Emperor Nero. Now, before closing, let me set before you briefly some general considerations drawn from the history of Roman Gaul which are applicable to universal history.

From what I have told you, it follows that the fortunes of peoples and states depend in part on what might be called the historic situation of every age, the situation that is created by the general state of the world in every successive epoch and which no people or state can mould at its own pleasure. Without doubt, a nation will never conquer a noteworthy greatness if the men that compose it fail of a certain culture, a certain energy, a social *morale* sufficiently vigorous; but though these qualities are necessary, they are not equally productive in all periods, but serve more or less, in different periods, according as general circumstances are disposed about a people. Gaul was fertile, and its people possessed before the conquest the qualities that they displayed later: and yet, as long as Gaul remained apart from the Empire, without continuous and numerous communications with the vast Mediterranean world; as long as it was split into so many petty rival states, occupied in serious wars against the Germanic tribes, its fertility remained hidden in the earth, and the ability of its inhabitants dissipated itself in devastating wars, instead of spending itself in fruitful effort. All that changed, and without any one's foresight or intent, when the Roman policy, urged by the internal forces that stirred the Republic, had destroyed that old order of things.

The ancients understood that peoples, like individual men, can regulate their destiny only in part; that about us, above us, are forces complex and obscure, which we can hardly comprehend, which invest us, seize us, impel us whither we had not thought to go, now to shipwreck on the rocks of misadventure, now to the discovery of islands of happiness, or to find, like Columbus, an America on the way to India. The Greeks called this power; the Latins, Fortuna, and deified it; erected temples and made sacrifices to it; dedicated to it a cult, of which Augustus was a devotee, and which contained more secret wisdom of life than all the superb theories on human destiny conceived by European genius in the delirium of this quarter-hour of measureless might in which we are living. No, man is not the voluntary artificer of his whole destiny; fortune and misfortune, triumph and catastrophe, are never entirely proportioned to personal merit or blame; every generation finds the world organised in a certain order of interests, forces, traditions, relations, and as it enjoys the good that preceding generations have accomplished, so in part it expiates the errors they have committed; as it draws advantage from beneficent forces acting outside of it and independent of its merit, so it suffers from the sinister forces that it finds — even though blameless itself — acting through the great mass of the world, among men and their works. From this relation to the unseen follows a rule of wisdom that modern men, full of unbounded pride, and persuaded that they are the beginning and end of the universe, too often forget: we must indeed press on with all our powers to the accomplishment of a great task, for although our destiny is never entirely made by our own hands, there is no destiny on the earth for the lazy; but, since a part of what we are depends not on ourselves, but upon what the ancients called Fortune, we dare never be too much elated over success, nor abased by failure. The wheel of destiny turns by a mysterious law, alike for families and for peoples: those in high position may fall; those in low, may rise.

Certainly Cæsar never suspected when he was fighting the Gauls, that the great-grandsons of the vanquished would live in villas modelled on the Roman, but more sumptuous; that the great Gallic nobles would have the satisfaction of parading before the people that conquered them a latinity more impressive and magnificent; and that some day the Gaul put by him to fire and sword would get the better, in empire, in wealth, in culture, of even Italy.

NERO

ON the 13th of October of 54 A.D., when Emperor Claudius died, the Senate chose as his successor his adopted son, Nero, a young man of seventeen, fat and short-sighted, who had until then studied only music, singing, and drawing. This choice of a child-emperor, who lacked imperial qualities and suggested the child kings of Oriental monarchies, was a scandalous novelty in the constitutional history of Rome. The ancient historians, especially Tacitus, considered the event as the result of an intrigue, cleverly arranged by Nero's mother, Agrippina, a daughter of Germanicus and granddaughter of Agrippa, the builder of the Pantheon. According to these historians, Agrippina, a highly ambitious woman, induced Claudius to marry her after Messalina's death, although she was a widow and had a child, and as soon as she entered the emperor's mansion she began to open the way for the election of her son. In order to exclude Britannicus, the son of Messalina, from succession, she persuaded Claudius to adopt Nero; then, with the help of the two tutors of the young man, Seneca and Burrhus, created in the Senate and among the Prætorians, a party favourable to her son; no sooner did she feel that she could rely on the Senate and the Prætorians, than she poisoned Claudius.

Too many difficulties prevent our accepting this version. To cite one of them will suffice: if Agrippina wished—as she surely did— that her son should succeed Claudius, she must also have wished that Claudius would live at least eight or ten years longer. As a great-grandson of Drusus, a grandson of Germanicus and the last descendant of his line, the only line in the whole family enjoying a real popularity, Nero was sure of election if he were of age at the death of Claudius. After the terrible scandal in which his mother had disappeared, Britannicus was no longer a competitor to be feared. There was only one danger for Nero, if Claudius should die too soon, the Senate might refuse to trust the Empire to a child.

I believe that Claudius died of disease, probably, if we can judge from Tacitus's account, of gastroenteritis, and that Agrippina's coterie, surprised by this sudden death, which upset all their plans, decided to put through Nero's election in spite of his youth, in order to insure the power to the line of Drusus, which had so much sympathy among the masses. As a matter of fact, the admiration for Drusus and his family triumphed over all other considerations: Nero became emperor at seventeen; but when the election was over, Rome—again according to the tales of the ancient historians—saw a still greater scandal than his election. The young man—and this is credible—hastened to engage as his master the first zither-player of Rome, Terpnos; continued his study of singing; and bought statues, pictures, bronzes, beautiful slaves, while his mother seized the actual control of the State.

Agrippina insisted on being kept informed of all affairs; directed the home and foreign policy; and if she did not reach the point of partaking in the sessions of the Senate, which would have been the supreme scandal, she called it to meet in her palace and, concealed behind a black curtain, listened to its discussions. In short, the Empire fell into the hands of a woman; Rome saw the evolution of customs, through which woman had for four centuries been freeing herself from her ancient slavery, suddenly a fact accomplished by her visible intervention in politics—the intervention that the great keepers of tradition, first among them Cato, had always decried as the most frightful cataclysm that could menace the city.

This story is also the exaggeration of a simpler truth. Even if Nero had been a very serious young man, at his age he could not by himself have governed the Empire; it would have been necessary for him to serve a long apprenticeship and to listen to experienced counsellors. Burrhus and Seneca, his two teachers, were naturally destined to be his counsellors; but why should not his mother also have helped him? Like all the women of her family, Agrippina was of superior mind, of high culture, and, as Tacitus himself admits, led a most respectable life, at least to the time of her marriage with Claudius. Brought up, as she was, in that family which for eighty years had been governing the Empire, she was well informed about affairs of State. Is it possible to suppose that such a woman would shut herself up in her home to weave wool, when, with her talent, her energy, her experience, she could be of so much service to her son and to the State? We do not need to attribute to Agrippina a monstrous ambition, as does Tacitus, in order to explain how the Empire was ruled during the first two years, by Seneca, Burrhus, and Agrippina; it was a natural consequence of the situation created by the premature death of Claudius. Tacitus himself is forced to recognise that the government was excellent.

Helping her son in the apprenticeship of the Empire, Agrippina did her duty; but during restless times when misunderstanding is almost a law of social life, it is often very dangerous to do one's duty. The period of Agrippina and Nero was full of confusion; though apparently quiet, Italy was deeply torn by the great struggle that gives the history of the Empire its marvellous character of actuality, the struggle between the old Roman military society and the intellectual civilisation of the Orient.

The ancient aristocratic and military Roman society had had so great and world-wide a success, that the ideas, the institutions and the customs, that had made it a perfect model of State, considered as an organ of political and military domination, exercised a great prestige on the following generations. Even during the time of which we speak, every one was forced after eight years of peace, to admit that the Empire had been created by those ideas, those institutions and those customs; that for the sake of the Empire they must be maintained, and alike in family as in State, must be opposed all that forms the essence of intellectual civilisation; that is to say, all that develops personal selfishness at the expense of collective interest—luxury, idleness, pleasure, celibacy, feminism, and at the same time, all that develops personality and intelligence at the expense of tradition—liberty of women, independence of children, variety of personal tendencies, and the critical spirit in all forms.

In spite of the resistance offered by traditions, peace and wealth favoured everywhere the diffusion of the intellectual civilisation of the Hellenised Orient. The woman now become free, and the intellectual man now become powerful, were the springs to set in motion this revolution. Under Claudius, in vain had they exiled Seneca, the brilliant philosopher and the peace-advocating humanitarian, who had diffused in high Roman society so many ideas and sentiments considered by the traditionalists pernicious to the force of the State; he had come back far more powerful, and ruled the Empire. Husbands, burdened by the excessive expenses, by the too frequent infidelities, by the tyrannical caprices of their wives, in vain regretted the good old time when husbands were absolute masters; the invading feminism weakened everywhere the strength of the aristocratic and military traditions.

So contradiction was everywhere. The Republic had still its old aristocratic constitution, but the nobility was no longer spurred by that absorbing and exclusive passion for politics and war, which had been its power. Society life, pleasure, amateur philosophy and literature, mysticism, and, above all, sports, dissipated in a thousand directions its energy and activity. Too many young men were to be found in the nobility who, like Nero, preferred singing, dancing, and driving, to caring for their clients or enduring the troubles of public office.

Augustus and Tiberius had done their utmost to strengthen the great Latin principle of parsimony in public and private life: in order to set a good example they had lived very simply; they had caused new sumptuary laws to be passed and tried to enforce the old ones; they had spent the State moneys, not for the keeping of artists and writers, nor for the building of monuments of useless size, but to build the great roads of the Empire, to strengthen the frontiers; they had made the public treasure into an aid fund for all suffering cities, stricken by earthquake, fire, or flood. And yet the Oriental influence, so favourable to unproductive and luxurious expenditure, gained ground steadily. The merchant of Syrian and Egyptian objects *de luxe,* in spite of the sumptuary laws, found a yearly increasing patronage in all the cities of Italy. The exactingness of the desire for public spectacles increased, even in secondary cities. The Italian people were losing their peasant's petty avarice and growing fond of things monumental and colossal, which was the great folly of the Orient. They found the monuments of Rome poor; everywhere, even in modest *municipia,* they demanded immense theatres, great temples, monumental basilicas, spacious forums, adorned with statues. In spite of the principles insisted upon with so much vigour by Augustus and Tiberius, public finances had, thanks to the weak Claudius and the extravagant Messalina, already gone through a period of great waste and disorder.

These contradictions, and the psychological disorder that followed, explain the discords and struggles very soon raging around the young Emperor. The public began to feel shocked by the attention that Agrippina gave to State affairs, as by a new and this time intolerable scandal of feminism. Agrippina was not a feminist, as a matter of fact, but a traditionalist, proud of the glory of her family, attached to the ancient Roman ideas, desirous only of seeing her son develop into a new Germanicus, a second Drusus. Solely the necessity of helping Nero had led her to meddle with politics. But not in vain had Cato declaimed so loudly in Rome against women who pretend to govern states; not in vain had Augustus's domination been at least partly founded on the great antifeminist legend of Antony and Cleopatra, which represented the fall of the great Triumvir as the consequence of a woman's influence. The public, although willing to give all possible freedom to women in other things, still remained quite firm on this point: politics must remain the monopoly of man. So to the popular imagination, Agrippina soon became a sort of Roman Cleopatra. Many interests gathered quickly to reinforce this antifeminist reaction, which, although exaggerated, had its origin in sincere feeling.

Agrippina, as a true descendant of Drusus, meant to prepare her son to rule the Empire according to the principles held by his great ancestors. Among these principles was to be counted not only the defence of Romanism and the maintenance of the aristocratic constitution, but also a wise economy in the management of finances. Agrippina is a good instance of that well-known fact— the British have noticed it more than once in India—that in public administration discreet and capable women keep, as a rule, the spirit of economy with which they manage the home. This is why, especially in despotic states, they rule better than men. Even before Claudius's death, Agrippina had vigorously opposed waste and plunder; it also appears that the reorganisation of finances after Messalina's death was due chiefly to her.

The continuation under Nero of this severe régime displeased a great number of persons, who dreamed of seeing again the easy sway of Messalina. From the moment they were satisfied that Agrippina, like Augustus and Tiberius, would not allow the public money to be stolen, many people found her insistent interference in public affairs unbearable. In short, Agrippina became unpopular, and, as always happens, because of faults she did not have. A noble deed, which she was trying to accomplish in defence of tradition, definitively compromised her situation.

Her son resembled neither Agrippina nor the great men of her family. He had a most indocile temperament, rebellious to tradition, in no sense Roman. Little by little, Agrippina saw the young Emperor develop into a precocious *debauché,* frightfully selfish, erratically vain, full of extravagant ideas, who, instead of setting the example of respect toward sumptuary laws, openly violated them all; and across whose mind from time to time flashed sinister lightnings of cruelty. Nero's youth—the fact is not surprising—

did not resist the mortal seductions of immense power and immense riches; but Agrippina, the proud granddaughter of the conqueror of Germany, must have chafed at the idea of her son's preferring musical entertainments to the sessions of the Senate, singing lessons to the study of tactics and strategy.

She applied herself, therefore, with all her energy to the work of tearing her son from his pleasures, and bringing about his return to the great traditions of his family. Nero resisted: the struggle between mother and son grew complicated; it excited the passion of the public, which felt that this conflict had a greater importance than any other family quarrel, that it was actually a struggle between traditional Romanism and Oriental customs. Unfortunately, every one sided with Nero: the sincere friends of tradition, because they did not want the rule of a woman, whoever she might be; those that longed for Messalina's times, because they saw personified in Agrippina the austere and inflexible spirit of the *gens Claudia*. The situation was soon without an issue. The accord of Agrippina with Seneca and Burrhus was troubled, because the two teachers of the young Emperor, under the impression of public malcontent, had somewhat withdrawn from her. Nero, who was sullen, cynical, and lazy, feared his mother too much to have the courage to oppose her openly, but he did not fear her enough to mend his ways. The mother, on her side, was set to do her duty to the end. Like all situations without an issue, this one was suddenly solved by an unexpected event.

Insisting on wanting to make a Roman of this young *debauché*, Agrippina made him into a murderer. Nero, progressing from one caprice to another, finally imagined a great folly: to divorce Octavia and to raise to her place a beautiful freedwoman called Acte. According to one of the fundamental laws of the State, the great law of Augustus on marriage, which forbade marriages between senators and freedwomen, the union of Nero and Acte could be only a concubinage. Agrippina wanted to avoid this scandal; and, as Nero persisted in his idea, it seems that she actually thought of having him deposed and of securing the choice of Britannicus, a very serious young man, as his successor. A true Roman, Agrippina was ready to sacrifice her son for the sake of the Republic.

The threat was, or appeared to be, so serious to Nero, that it made him step over the threshold of crime. One day during a great dinner to which he had been invited by Nero, Britannicus was suddenly seized with violent convulsions. "It is an attack of epilepsy," said Nero calmly, giving orders to his slaves to remove Britannicus and care for him. The young man died in a few hours and every one believed that Nero had poisoned him.

This dastardly crime aroused at first a sense of horror and fright among the people, but the impression did not last long. In spite of all his faults, Nero was liked. In Rome they had respected Augustus and hated Tiberius; they had killed Caligula and jeered at Claudius; Nero seemed to be the first of the Roman Emperors who stood a chance of becoming popular. Contrary to Agrippina's ideas, it was his frivolity that pleased the great masses, because this frivolity corresponded to the slow but progressive decay of the old Roman virtues in them. They expected from Nero a less hard, less severe, less parsimonious government—in a word, a government less Roman than the rule of his predecessors, a government which, instead of force, glory, and wisdom, meant pleasure and ease.

So it happened that many soon forgot the unfortunate Britannicus, and some even tried to justify Nero by invoking State necessity. Agrippina alone remained the object of the universal hatred, as the sole cause of so many misfortunes. Implacable enemies, concealed in the shadow, were subtly at work against her; they organised a compaign of absurd calumnies in the Court itself, and it is this campaign from which Tacitus drew his material.

Some wretches finally dared even accuse her of conspiracy against the life of her son. Agrippina, refusing to plead for herself, still weathered the storm, because Nero was afraid of her, and though he tried to escape from her authority, did not dare to initiate any energetic move against her. To engage in a final struggle with so indomitable a woman, another woman was necessary. This woman was Poppæa Sabina, a very handsome and able dame of the great Roman nobility. Poppæa represented Oriental feminism in its most dangerous form: a woman completely demoralised by luxury, elegance, society life, and voluptuousness, who eluded all her duties toward the species in order to enjoy and make others enjoy her beauty.

Corrupted as that age was, Poppæa was more corrupt. As soon as she observed the strong impression she had made on Nero, she conceived the plan of becoming his wife; her beauty would then be admired by the whole Empire, would be surrounded by a luxury for which the means of her husband were not sufficient, and with which no other Roman dame could compete. There was one obstacle—Agrippina.

Agrippina protected Octavia, a true Roman woman, simple and honest: Agrippina would never consent to this absolutely unjustifiable divorce. To force Nero to a decisive move against his mother, Poppæa had her husband sent on some mission to Lusitania and became the mistress of the Emperor. From that point the situation changed. Dominated by Poppæa's influence, Nero found the courage to force Agrippina to abandon his palace and seek refuge in Antony's house; he took from her the privilege of Prætorian guards, which he himself had granted her; he reduced to a minimum the number and time of his visits, and carefully avoided being left alone with her. Agrippina's influence, to the general satisfaction, rapidly declined, while Nero gained every day in popularity. Agrippina, however, was too energetic a woman peaceably to resign herself: she began a violent campaign against the two adulterers, which deeply troubled the public. In Rome, where Augustus had promulgated his stern law against adultery; in Rome, where Augustus himself had been obliged to submit to his own law, when he exiled his daughter and his granddaughter and almost exterminated the whole family; in Rome, a young man of twenty-two dared all but officially introduce adultery and polygamy into the Palatine! In her struggle against Nero, Agrippina once more stood on tradition: and Nero was afraid.

Poppæa was probably the one who suggested to Nero the idea of killing Agrippina. The idea had been, as it were, floating in the air for a long time, because Agrippina was embarrassing to many persons and interests. It was chiefly the party that wanted to sack the imperial budget, to introduce the finance of great expenditure, which could not tolerate this clever and energetic woman, who was so faithful to the great traditions of Augustus and Tiberius, who could neither be frightened nor corrupted. One should not consider the assassination of Agrippina as a simple personal crime of Nero, as the result of his and Poppæa's quarrels with his mother. This crime, besides personal causes, had a political origin. Nero would never have dared commit such a misdeed, in the eyes of the Roman almost a sacrilege, if he had not been encouraged by Agrippina's unpopularity, by the violent hatred of so many against his mother.

Nero hesitated long; he decided only when his freedman, Anicetus, the commander of the fleet, proposed a plan that seemed to guarantee secrecy for the crime: to have a ship built with a concealed trap. It was the spring of the year 59 A.D.; the Court had moved to Baiæ, on the Gulf of Naples. If Nero succeeded in getting his mother on board the vessel, Anicetus would take upon himself the task of burying quickly below the waves the secret of her death; the people who hated Agrippina would easily be satisfied with the explanations to be given them.

Nero executed his part of the plan in perfect cold-blood. He made believe he had repented and was anxious for a reconciliation with his mother; he invited her to Baiæ and so profusely lavished kindnesses and amiabilities upon her, that Agrippina finally believed in his sincerity.

After spending a few days at Baiæ, Agrippina decided to return to Antium; in a very happy frame of mind and full of hopes that her son would soon show himself to the world the man she had dreamed, the descendant of Drusus, she boarded one evening the fatal ship; Nero had escorted her thither and pressed her to his heart with the most demonstrative tenderness.

A calm night diffused its starry shadows over the quiet sea, which with subdued murmur lulled in their sleep the great summer homes along the shore. The ship departed, carrying toward her sombre destiny Agrippina, absorbed in her smiling dreams. When the moment came and the wrecking machine was set to work, the vessel did not sink as fast as they had hoped: it listed, overturning people and things. Agrippina had time to understand the danger; with admirable presence of mind she jumped overboard and escaped by swimming, while, during the confusion on the boat, the hired murderers killed one of Agrippina's freedwomen, mistaking her for Agrippina herself. The ship finally sank; the murderers also took to the water; everything returned to its wonted calm; the starry night still diffused its silent shadows; the sea still cradled with subdued murmur the homes along the coast —all men slept except one.

Within this one, Anxiety watched: a son was awaiting the news that his mother was dead, and that he was free to celebrate a criminal marriage. The escaped murderers soon brought the news so impatiently expected—but Nero's joy was short. At dawn, a freedman of Agrippina arrived at the Emperor's villa. Agrippina, picked up by a boat, had succeeded in reaching one of her villas near by; she sent the freedman to tell the Emperor about the accident and to assure him of her safety.

Agrippina alive! It was like a thunderbolt to Nero, and he lost his head: he saw his mother hurrying on to Rome, denouncing the abominable attempt to Senate and people, rousing against him the Prætorian guard and the legions. Thoroughly frightened, he summoned Seneca and Burrhus and laid before them the terrible situation. It is easy to imagine the shock of the old preceptors. How could he risk such a grave imprudence? And yet there was no time to lose in reproaches. Nero begged for advice: Seneca and Burrhus were silent, but they, also frightened, asked of themselves what Agrippina would do. Would she not provoke a colossal scandal, which would ruin everything? An expedient, the same one, occurred to both of them: but so sinister was the idea that they dared not speak it. This time, however, both the philosopher and the general were deceived as well as Nero: Agrippina had guessed the truth and given up the struggle. What could she, a lone woman do against an Emperor who did not stop even at the plan of murdering his mother? She realised, during that awful night, that only one chance of safety was left to her—to ignore what had taken place; and she sent her freedman with the message that meant forgiveness. But fear kept Nero and his counsellors from understanding; and when they could easily have remedied the preceding mistake, they compromised all by a supreme error. Finally Seneca, the pacificator and humanitarian philosopher, thought he had found the way of making half-openly the only suggestion which seemed wise to him: he turned to Burrhus and asked what might happen, if an order were given the Prætorians to kill Nero's mother. Burrhus understood that his colleague, although the first to give the fatal advice, was trying to shift upon him the much more serious responsibility of carrying it out; since, if they reached the decision of having Agrippina disposed of by the Prætorians, no one but he, the commander of the guard, could utter the order. He therefore protested with the greatest energy that the Prætorians would never lay murderous hands on the daughter of Germanicus. Then he added cogitatively that, if it were thought necessary, Anicetus and his sailors could finish the work already begun. Thus Burrhus gave the same advice as Seneca, but he, like his colleague, meant to pass on to some one else the task of execution. He chose better than Seneca: Anicetus, if Agrippina lived, ran a serious risk of becoming the scapegoat of all this affair. In fact, as soon as Nero gave his assent, Anicetus and a few sailors hastened to the villa of Agrippina and stabbed her.

The crime was abominable. Nero and his circle were so awed by it that they attempted to make the people believe that Agrippina had committed suicide, when her conspiracy against her son's life had been discovered. This was the official version of Agrippina's death, sent by Nero to the Senate. But this audacious mystification had no success. The public divined the truth, and roused by the voice of their age-long instincts, they cried out that the Emperor no less than any peasant of Italy must revere his father and his mother. Through a sudden turn of public feeling, Agrippina, who had been so much hated during her life, became the object of a kind of popular veneration; Nero, on the other hand, and Poppæa inspired a sentiment of profound horror.

If Nero had found the living Agrippina unbearable, he soon realised that his dead mother was much more to be feared. In fact, scared as he was by the popular agitation, not only had he temporarily to give up the plan of divorcing Octavia and marrying Poppæa, but felt obliged to stay several months at Baiæ, not daring to return to Rome. He was, however, no longer a child: he was twenty-three years old and had some talent. Men of intelligence and energy were also not wanting in his *entourage*. The first shock once over, the Emperor and his coterie rallied. The first impression had indeed been disastrous, but had brought about no irreparable consequences—the only consequences that count in politics. One could therefore hope that the public would gradually forget this murder as they had forgotten that of Britannicus. One only needed to help them forget. Nero resolved to give Italy and Rome the administrative revolution that had found in Agrippina so determined an opponent, the easy, splendid, generous government that seemed to suit the popular taste.

He began by organising among the *jeunesse dorée* of Rome the "festivals of youth." In these true demonstrations against the old aristocratic education, now in the house of one and then in the garden of another, the young patricians met under the Emperor's directions. They sang, recited, and danced, displaying all the tendencies that tradition held unworthy of a Roman nobleman. Later, Nero built in the Vatican fields a private stadium, where he amused himself with driving, and invited his friends to join him. He surrounded himself with poets, musicians, singers; enormously increased the budget of popular festivals; planned and started immense constructions; introduced into all parts of the administration a new spirit of carelessness and ease. Not only the sumptuary laws, but all laws commanding the fulfilment of human duties toward the species, such as the great laws of Augustus on marriage and adultery, were no longer applied; the surveillance of the Senate over the governors, that of the governors over the cities, slackened. In Rome, in all Italy, in the provinces, the treasuries of the Republic, the possessions and the funds of the cities, were robbed. In the midst of this unbridled plundering, which appeared to make every man rich quickly, and without work, a delirium of luxury and pleasure reigned: in Rome especially, people lived in a continuous orgy; the nobility answered in crowds the invitations of Nero; the Senate, the great houses, where the conquerors of the world had been born, swarmed with young athletes and drivers, who had no other ambition but that of adding the prize of a race to the war trophies of their ancestors; the imperial palace was invaded by a noisy horde of zitherists, actors, jockeys, athletes, among whom Burrhus and, still more, Seneca, were beginning to feel most ill at ease.

Agrippina's death, even though it had yet deferred Nero's marrying Poppæa, had made possible the change in the government that a part of the people wished. We owe to this new principle the immense ruins of ancient Rome; but this fact does not authorise us to consider it a Roman principle: it was, instead, a principle of Oriental civilisation which had forced itself upon the Roman traditions after a long and painful effort. The revolution, however, had been long preparing and corresponded to the popular aspirations. It would, therefore, have redounded to the advantage of the Emperor, who had dared to break loose from a superannuated tradition, had not Agrippina's spectre still haunted Rome. To their honour be it said, the people of Rome and Italy had not yet become so corrupted by Oriental civilisation as to forget parricide in a few festivals.

The party of tradition, though weakened, existed. They began a brave fight against Nero, using the assassination of Agrippina as the adverse party had exploited the antifeminist prejudices of the masses against Agrippina herself. They denounced the parricide to the people, in order to attack the champion of Orientalism and irritate against him the indifferent mass, which, not understanding the great struggle between the Orient and Rome, remained unstirred. Hoping the excitement of spirit had somewhat subsided, Nero had finally carried out his old plan of divorcing Octavia and marrying Poppæa; but the divorce caused great popular demonstrations in Rome in favour of the abused wife and against the intruder.

Moreover, thanks to his extravagance, Nero made things very easy for his enemies, the defenders of tradition. His habits of dissipation exaggerated all the faults of his character, chiefly his morbid need of showing himself off, of defying the public, their prejudices, their opinions. It is difficult to discern how much is true and how much is false in the hideous stories of debauchery handed down to us by the ancient writers, particularly Suetonius.

Although one might believe — and I believe it for my part — that there is a great deal of exaggeration in such tales, it is certain that Nero's personality played too conspicuous a part in his administrative revolution. Ready as the people were to admire a more generous and luxurious government than that of Augustus, Tiberius, and Claudius, they still liked to look to the chief of State as to a man of gravity and austerity, who let others amuse themselves, though he himself be bored. The vain and bizarre young man, who was always the guest of honour at his own *fêtes*, who never hesitated to satisfy his most extravagant caprices, who spent so much money to divert himself, shocked the last republican susceptibilities of Italy. The wise felt alarmed: with such expenses, would it not all end in bankruptcy? For all these causes, they soon began to reproach Nero for his prodigality, although the people enjoyed it, just as they had been malcontent with Tiberius for his parsimony. His caprices, ever stranger, little by little roused even that part of the public which was not fanatically attached to tradition. At that time Nero developed his foolish vanity of actor, his caprice for the theatre, which soon was to become an all-absorbing mania. The chief of the Empire, the heir of Julius

Cæsar, dreamed of nothing else than descending from the height of human grandeur to the scene of a theatre, to experience before the public the sensations of those players whom the Roman nobility had always regarded as instruments of infamous pleasure!

Disgusted with Nero's mismanagement and follies, Seneca took the death of Burrhus as an opportunity to retire. Then Nero, freed from the last person who still retained any influence over him, gave himself up entirely to the insane swirl of his caprices. He ended one day by presenting himself in the theatre of Naples. Naples was yet then a Greek city. Nero had chosen it for this reason; he was applauded with frenzy. But the Italians of the other cities protested: the chief of the Empire appearing in a theatre, his hand on the zither and not on the sword! Imagine what would be the impression if some day a sovereign went on the stage of the *folies Bergères* as a "number" for a sleight-of-hand performance!

Public attention, however, was turned from this immense scandal by a frightful calamity—the famous conflagration of Rome, which began the nineteenth of July of the year 64 and devastated almost all quarters of the city for ten days. What was the cause of the great disaster? This very obscure point has much interested historians, who have tried in vain to throw light on the subject. As far as I am concerned, I by no means exclude the hypothesis that the fire might have been accidental. But when they are crushed under the weight of a great misfortune, men always feel sure that they are the victims of human wickedness: a sad proof of their distrust in their fellow men. The plebs, reduced to utter misery by the disaster, began to murmur that mysterious people had been seen hurrying through the different quarters, kindling the fire and cumbering the work of help; these incendiaries must have been sent by some one in power—by whom?

A strange rumour circulated: Nero himself had ordered the city to be burned, in order to enjoy a unique sight, to get an idea of the fire of Troy, to have the glory of rebuilding Rome on a more magnificent scale. The accusation seems to me absurd. Nero was a criminal, but he was not a fool to the point of provoking the wrath of the whole people for so light a motive, especially after Agrippina's death. Tacitus himself, in spite of his hatred of all Cæsar's family and his readiness to make them responsible for the most serious crimes, does not venture to express belief in this story —sufficient proof that he considers it absurd and unlikely. Nevertheless, the hatred that surrounded Nero and Poppæa made every one, not only among the ignorant populace, but also among the higher classes, accept it readily. It was soon the general opinion that Nero had accomplished what Brennus and Catiline's conspirators could not do. Was a more horrible monster ever seen? Parricide, actor, incendiary!

The traditionalist party, the opposition, the unsatisfied, exploited without scruple this popular attitude, and Nero, responsible for a sufficient number of actual crimes, found himself accused also of an imaginary one. He was so frightened that he decided to give the clamouring people a victim, some one on whom Rome could avenge its sorrow. An inquiry into the causes of the conflagration was ordered. The inquest came to a strange conclusion. The fire had been started by a small religious sect, recently imported from the Orient, a sect whose name most people then learned for the first time: the Christians.

How did the Roman authorities come to such a conclusion? That is one of the greatest mysteries of universal history, and no one will ever be able to clear it. If the explanation of the disaster as accepted by the people was absurd, the official explanation was still more so. The Christian community of Rome, the pretended volcano of civil hatred, which had poured forth the destructive fire over the great metropolis, was a small and peaceful congregation of pious idealists.

A great and simple man, Paul of Tarsus, had taken up again among them the great work in which Augustus and Tiberius had failed: he aimed at the remaking of popular conscience, but used means until then unknown in the Græco-Latin civilisation. Not in the name of the ancestors, of the traditions, of ideals of political power, did he seek to persuade men to work, to refrain from vice, to live honestly and simply; but in the name of a single God, whom man had in the beginning offended through his pride, in the name of the Son of God, who had taken human form and volunteered to die as a criminal on the cross, to appease the Father's wrath against the rebellious creature. On the Græco-Roman idea of duty, Paul grafted the Christian idea of sin. Doubtless the new theology must have seemed at first obscure to Greeks and Romans; but Paul put into it that new spirit, mutual love, which the dry Latin soul had hardly ever known, and he vivi-fied it with the example of an obscure life of sacrifice.

Paul was born of a noble Hebrew family of Tarsus, and was a man of high culture. He had, to use a modern expression, simplified him-self, renounced his position in a time when few could resist the pas-sion for luxury, and taken up a trade for his living; with the scanty profit from his work as a tent-maker, alone and on foot he made measureless journeys through the Empire, everywhere preaching the redemption of man. Finally, after numberless adventures and perils, he had come to Rome and had, in the great city frenzied by the delirium of luxury and pleasure, repeated to the poor, who alone were willing to hear him: "Be chaste and pure, do not deceive each other, love one another, help one another, love God."

If Nero had known the little society of pious idealists, he surely would have hated it, but for other motives than the imaginary accusations of his police. In this story St. Paul is exactly the antithesis of Nero. The latter represents the atrocious selfishness of rich, peaceful, highly civilised epochs; the former, the ardent moral idealism which tries to react against the cardinal vices of power and wealth through universal self-sacrifice and asceticism. Neither of these men is to be comprehended without the other, because the moral doctrine of Paul is partly a reaction against the violent folly for which Nero stood the symbol; but it certainly was not philosophical considerations of this kind that led the Roman authorities to rage against the Christians. The problem, I repeat, is insoluble. However this may be, the Christians were declared responsible for the fire; a great number were taken into custody, sentenced to death, executed in different ways, during the festivals that Nero offered to the people to appease them. Possibly Paul himself was one of the victims of this persecution.

This diversion, however, was of no use. The conflagration definitely ruined Nero. With the conflagration begins the third period of his life, which lasts four years. It is characterised by absurd exaggerations of all kinds, which hastened the inevitable catastrophe. One grandiose idea dominates it: the idea of building on the ruins a new Rome, immense and magnificent, a true metropolis for the Empire. In order to carry out this plan, Nero did not economise; he began to spend in it the moneys laid aside to pay the legions. The people of Italy, however, and even of Rome, which grew rich on these public expenditures, did not show themselves thankful for this immense architectural effort. Every one was sure that the new city would be worse than the old one!

Nero himself, exasperated by this invincible hate, exhausted by his own excesses, lost what reason he had still left, and his government degenerated into a complete tyranny, suspicious, violent, and cruel.

Piso's conspiracy caused him to order a massacre of patricians, which left terrible rancour in its wake; in an access of fury, he killed Poppæa; he began to imagine accusations against the richest men of the Empire, in order to confiscate their estates. His prodigality and the general carelessness had completely disorganised the finances of the Empire; he had to recur to all kinds of expedients to find money. Finally he undertook a great artistic tour in Greece—that province which had been the mother of arts —to play in its most celebrated theatres. This time indignation burst all bounds. The armies of Gaul and Spain, for a long time irregularly paid, led by their officers, revolted. This act of energy sufficed. On the 9th of June, 68 A.D., abandoned by all the world, Nero was compelled to commit suicide.

So the family of Julius Cæsar disappears from history. After so much greatness, genius, and wisdom, the fall may seem petty and almost laughable. It is absurd to lose the Empire for the pleasure of singing in a theatre. And yet, bizarre as the end may seem, it was not the result of the vices, the follies, and the crimes of Nero alone. In his way, Nero himself was, like all members of his family, the victim of the contradictory situation of his times.

It has been repeated for centuries, that the foundation of monarchy was the great mission of Cæsar's family. I believe this to be a great mistake. The lot of the family would have been simple and easy, if it had been able to found a monarchy. The family of Cæsar had to solve another problem, much more difficult,—in fact insoluble; a problem that may be compared, from a certain point of view, to that which confronted the Bonapartes in the nineteenth century. The Bonapartes found old monarchical, legitimistic, theocratic Europe agitated by forces which, although making it impossible for the ancient régime to continue, were not yet able to establish a new society, entirely democratic, republican, and lay. The family of Cæsar found the opposite situation: an old military and aristocratic republic, which was changing into an intellectual and monarchical civilisation, based on equality, but opposing formidable resistance to the forces of transformation. In these situations the two families tried in all ways to reconcile things not to be conciliated, to realise the impossible: one, the popular monarchy and imperial democracy; the other, the monarchical republic and Orientalised Latinity. The contradiction was for both families the law of life, the cause of greatness; this explains why neither was ever willing to extricate itself from it, in spite of the advice of philosophers, the malcontent of the masses, the pressure of parties, and the evident dangers. This contradiction was also the fatality of both families, the cause of their ruin; it explains the shortness of their power, their restless existence, and the continuous catastrophes that opened the way to the final crash.

Waterloo and Sedan, the exile of Julia and the tragic failure of Tiberius's government, all the misfortunes great and small which struck the two families, were always consequences of the insoluble contradiction they tried to solve. You have had a perfectly characteristic example of it in the brief story I have been telling you.

Agrippina becomes an object of universal hatred and dies by assassination because she defends tradition; her son disregards tradition and, chiefly for this very reason, is finally forced to kill himself. Doubtless the fate of the Bonapartes is less tragic, because they, at least, escaped the infamous legend created by contemporary hatred against Cæsar's family, and artfully developed by the historians of successive generations. I hope to be able to prove in the continuation of my *Greatness and Decline of Rome,* that the history of Cæsar's family, as it has been told by Tacitus and Suetonius, is a sensational novel, a legend containing not much more truth than the legend of Atrides. The family of Cæsar, placed in the centre of the great struggle going on in Rome between the old Roman militarism, and the intellectual civilisation of the Orient, between nationalism and cosmopolitism, between Asiatic mysticism and traditional religion, between egoism over-excited by culture and wealth, and the supreme interests of the species, had to injure too many interests, to offend too many susceptibilities. The injured interests, the offended susceptibilities, revenged themselves through defaming legends.

The case of Nero is particularly instructive. He was half insane and a veritable criminal: it would be absurd to attempt in his favour the historical rehabilitation to which other members of the family, Tiberius for instance, have a right. And yet it has not been enough for succeeding generations that he atoned for his follies and crimes by death and infamy. They have fallen upon his memory: they have overlooked that extenuating circumstance of considerable importance, his age when elected; they have gone so far as to make him into a unique monster, no longer human and even the Antichrist!

Surely he first shed Christian blood; but if we consider the tendency he represented in Roman history, we can hardly classify him among the great enemies of Christianity. Unwittingly, Augustus and Tiberius were two great enemies of the Christian teachings, because they sought by all means to reinforce Roman tradition, and struggled against everything that would one day form the essence of Christianity—cosmopolitism, mysticism, the domination of intellectual people, the influence of the philosophical and metaphysical spirit on life. Nero, on the contrary, with his repeated efforts to spread Orientalism in Rome, and chiefly with his taste for art, was unconsciously a powerful collaborator of future Christian propaganda. We must not forget this: the masses in the Empire became Christian only because they had first been imbued with the Oriental spirit.

Nero and St. Paul, the man that wished to enjoy all, and the man that suffered all, are in their time two extreme antitheses: with the passing of centuries, they become two collaborators. While one suffered hunger and persecution to preach the doctrine of redemption, the other called to Italy and to Rome, to amuse himself, the goldsmiths, weavers, sculptors, painters, architects, musicians, whom Rome had always rebuffed.

Both disappeared, cut off by the violent current of their epoch; centuries went by: the name of the Emperor grew infamous, while that of the tent-maker radiated glory. In the midst of the immense disorder that accompanied the dissolution of the Roman Empire, as the bonds among men relaxed, and the human mind seemed to be incapable of reasoning and understanding, the disciples of the saint realised that the goldsmiths, weavers, sculptors, painters, architects, and musicians of the Emperor could collect the masses around the churches and make them patiently listen to what they could still comprehend of Paul's sublime morality. When you regard St. Mark or Notre Dame or any other stupendous cathedral of the Middle Ages, like museums for the work of art they hold, you see the luminous symbol of this paradoxical alliance between victim and executioner.

Only through the alliance of Paul and Nero could the Church dominate the disorder of the Middle Ages, and, from antiquity to the modern world, carry through that formidable storm the essential principles from which our civilisation developed: a decisive proof that, if history in its details is a continuous strife, as a whole it is the inevitable final reconciliation of antagonistic forces, obtained in spite of the resistance of individuals and by sacrificing them.

JULIA AND TIBERIUS

"He walked with head bent and fixed, the face stern, a taciturn man exchanging no word with those about him. . . . Augustus realised these severe and haughty manners, and more than once tried to excuse them in the Senate and to the people, saying that they were defects of temperament, not signs of a sinister spirit."

This is the picture that Suetonius gives us of Tiberius, the man who, in 9 B.C., after the death of Agrippa and Drusus, stood next to Augustus, his right hand and pre-established successor. At that time Augustus was fifty-four years old; not an old man, but he was ill and had presided over the Republic for twenty-one years. Many people must have asked themselves what would happen if Augustus should die, or should definitely retire to private life. The answer was not uncertain: since Rome was engaged in the conquest of Germany, the chief of the Empire and of the army ought to be a valiant general and a man of expert acquaintance with Germanic affairs. Tiberius was the first general of his time and knew Germany and the Germans better than any other Roman.

The passage from Suetonius, just quoted, indicates that Tiberius was not altogether popular, yet it was the accepted opinion that Rome and Italy might well be content to rely upon so capable a general and diplomat, if Augustus failed. This attitude, however, changed when the death of Drusus entirely removed the alternative of choice between himself and Tiberius, and the latter, up to that time universally admired, began to be met, even among the nobility, by a strong opposition. How can this apparently inexplicable fact be made clear? The theory of corruption so dear to

77

the ancients, which I have already explained, gives us the key to the mystery. Those who have been disposed to see in that theory merely a plaything of poets, orators, philosophers, will now realise that it had power enough to kill the person and destroy the family of the first citizen of the Empire. That kind of continuous fear of luxury, of amusements, of prodigality, on account of which the ancients called corruption so many things that we define as progress, was not a sentiment always equally alive in the mind of the multitude. The Romans, like ourselves, loved to live and to enjoy; this is so true that philosophers and legislators constantly took pains to remind them of the danger of allowing too much liberty to the appetites; but more effective than the counsels of philosophers and the threats of the law, great public calamities inspired in the masses, at least temporarily, a spirit of puritanism and austerity. Of this the consequences of the battle of Actium afforded noteworthy proof.

Those who have read the fourth volume of *The Greatness and Decline of Rome* may perhaps remember how I have described the conservative and traditionalist movement of the first decade of the government of Augustus. Frightened by the revolution, men's minds had reverted precipitously to the past. A new party, which one might call the traditionalist, had sought to re-establish the old-time order, in the state, in customs, in ideas; to combat the corruption of customs; and of this party Augustus had been the right arm. Indeed, to so great an extent had this party stirred up public spirit and prevailed upon those in power that in 18 B.C. it succeeded in passing some great social laws on luxury, on matrimony, on dress. With these laws, Rome proposed to remake, by terrible measures, the old, prolific, austere nobility of the aristocratic era. The *lex de maritandis ordinibus* aimed with a thousand vexatious restrictions to constrain the nobility to marry and have children; the *lex sumptuaria* studied to restrain extravagance; the *lex de adulteriis* proclaimed martial law in the family, menacing an unfaithful wife and her accomplice with exile for life and the confiscation of half their substance; legislation of the harshest, this, which should scourge Rome to blood, to keep her from falling anew into the inveterate vices from which the civil wars were born.

The impression of the civil wars could not last forever. In fact, in the decade that followed the promulgation of the social laws, the puritan fervour, which had up to that time heated all Italy, began to cool. Wealth increased; the confidence that order and peace were actually re-established, spread everywhere; the generation that had seen the civil wars, disappeared; peace and growing prosperity stirred in the next generation a desire for freedom and pleasure that would not endure the narrow traditionalism and the puritanism of the preceding generation; consequently also the laws of 18 B.C. became intolerable.

To understand this change in public spirit which had such serious consequences, there is no better way than by studying the most celebrated writer of this new generation, Ovid, who represents it most admirably both in life and works. Ovid was born at Sulmona in 43 B.C. He was about the same age as Tiberius,—of a knight's family—that is, of the wealthy middle class. He was destined by his father to the study of oratory and jurisprudence, evidently to make a political man of him, a senator, a future consul or proconsul, and to contribute to the great national restoration that his generation proposed to itself and of which Augustus was architect, preparing a new family for the political aristocracy that was governing the Empire. Ovid's father had all the requirements demanded by law and custom: a considerable fortune, the half-nobility of the equestrian order, an intelligent son, the means to give him the necessary culture—a favourable combination of circumstances which was wholly undone by a bit of unforeseen contrariety, the son's invincible inclination for what his father called, with little respect, a "useless study," literature. The young man had indifferently studied oratory and law, gone to Rome, married, made friendships in the high society of the capital, been elected to the offices preceding the quæstorship; but when the time arrived for presenting himself as candidate for the quæstorship itself—

that is, the time for beginning the true *curriculum* of the magistracies, he had declared that he would rather be a great poet than a consul, and there was no persuading him farther on the long road opened to political ambitions.

With the episode of Julia and Tiberius in mind, I have stated that Ovid's life epitomises the new generation, because it shows us in action the first of the forces that dissolved the aristocratic government and the nobility artificially reconstituted by Augustus at the close of the civil wars—intellectualism. The case of Ovid demonstrates that intellectual culture, literature, poetry, instead of being, for the Roman aristocracy, as in older times, a simple ornament, secondary to politics, had already a prime attraction for the man of genius; that even among the higher classes, devoted by tradition only to military and political life, there appeared, by the side of the leaders in war and politics, the professional literary man. The study of Ovid's work shows something even more noteworthy: that, profiting by the discords in the ruling class, these literary men feared no longer to express and to reenforce the discontent, the bad feeling, the aversion, that the efforts of the State to re-establish a more vigorous social order was rousing in one part of the public.

Ovid's first important work was the *Amores,* which was certainly out by the year 8 B.C., although in a different form from that in which we now have it. To understand what this book really was when it was published, one must remember that it was written, read, and what is more, *admired,* ten years after the promulgation of the *lex de maritandis ordinibus* and of the *lex de adulteriis;* it should be read with what remains of the text of those laws in hand.

We are astonished at the book, full of excitements to frivolity, to dissipation, to pleasure, to those very activities that appeared to the ancients to form the most dangerous part of the "corruption." Extravagances of a libertine poet? The single-handed revolt of a corrupt youth, which cannot be considered a sign of the times? No. If there had not been in the public at large, in the higher classes, in the new generation, a general sympathy with this poetry, subversive of the solemn Julian laws, Ovid would never have been recognised in the houses of the great, petted and admired by high society. The great social laws of Augustus, the publication of which had been celebrated by Horace in the *Carmen Seculare,* wounded too many interests, tormented too many selfishnesses, intercepted too many liberties. His revolutionary elegies had made Ovid famous, because these interests and these selfishnesses finally rebelled with the new generation, which had not seen the civil wars. Other incidents before and after the publication of the *Amores* also show this reaction against the social laws. Therefore Augustus proposed about this time to abolish the provision of the *lex de maritandis ordinibus* that excluded celibates from public spectacles; and by his personal intervention sought to put a check upon the scandalous trials for adultery that his law had originated — two acts that were so much admired by a part of the public that statues were erected to him by popular subscription.

In short, this new movement of public opinion explains the opposition exerted from this time on against Tiberius and makes us understand how there arose the conflict in which this mysterious personage was to be entangled for the rest of his life, and to lose, by no fault of his own, so great a part of his reputation. I hope to prove that the Tiberius of Tacitus and Suetonius is a fantastic personality, the hero of a wretched and improbable romance, invented by party hatred; that Tiberius remained, as a German historian has defined it, an undecipherable enigma, simply because there has never been the will to recognise how much alive the aristocratic republican traditions still were, and what force they still exerted in the State and in the family.

Tiberius was but an authentic Claudius — that is, a true descendant of one of the oldest, the proudest, the most aristocratic families of the Roman nobility, a man with all the good qualities and all the defects of the old Roman aristocracy, a man who regarded things and men with the eyes of a senator of the times of Scipio Africanus — a living anachronism, a fossil, if you will, from a bygone age, in a world that wished to tolerate no more either the vices or the virtues of the old aristocracy. He thought that the Empire ought to be governed by a limited aristocracy of diplomats and warriors, rigidly authoritative, exclusively Roman, which should know how to check the general corrupting of customs, the current extravagance and dissipation, beginning its task by imposing upon itself an inexorable self-discipline. Even though he belonged to the generation of Ovid—to the generation that had not seen the civil wars—Tiberius, by singular exception, kept aloof from the undisciplined frivolity of his contemporaries. He desired the severe application of the social laws of the year 18, as of all the traditional norms of aristocratic discipline. His generation therefore soon found him an enemy, especially after Drusus's death seemed to leave neither doubt nor choice as to the successor of Augustus. From this contemporary attitude arises the tacit aversion in the midst of which, after the lapse of so many centuries, we still feel Tiberius living and working, an aversion which steadily grows even while he renders the most signal services to the Empire.

There was between him and his generation irreconcilable discord. However, it is not likely that this blind and secret hatred alone could have seriously injured Tiberius, whose power and merits were so great, if it had not been considerably helped by incidents of various nature. The first and most important of these was the discord that had arisen, shortly after the death of Drusus, between Tiberius and his wife Julia, the daughter of Augustus and the widow of Agrippa.

Tiberius had married her against his will in the year 11, after the death of Agrippa, by order of Augustus, and had at first tried to live in accord with her; the attempt was vain, and the spirits of the husband and wife were soon parted in fatal disagreement. "He lived at first," writes Suetonius, "in harmony with Julia; but soon grew cool toward her, and finally the estrangement reached such a point after the death of their boy born at Aquilea, that Tiberius lived in a separate apartment"—a separation, as we would call it, in "bed and board." What was the reason of this discord? No ancient historian has revealed it; however, we can guess with sufficient probability from what we know of the characters of the pair and the discord that divided Roman society. If Tiberius was not the monster of Capri, Julia was certainly not the miserable Bacchante of the scandalous Roman chronicle. Macrobius has pictured her in human lights and shadows, a probable image, describing her as a highly cultured woman, lavish in tastes and expenditure, fond of beautiful literature, of the fine arts, and of the company of handsome and elegant young men. She belonged to the new generation of which Ovid was spokesman and poet; while Tiberius represented archaic traditionalism, the spirit of a past generation.

It is easy to understand how these two persons, incarnating the irreconcilable opposition of two epochs, two *morales*, two societies, of Roman militarism and of Oriental culture, could not live together. A man like Tiberius, severe, simple, who detested frivolous pleasures, caring more for war than for society life, could not live in peace with this beautiful and vivacious creature, who loved luxury, prodigality, brilliant company. It is not rash to suppose that the *lex sumptuaria* of the year 18 was the first grave cause of disagreement. Julia, given, as Macrobius describes her, to profuse expenditure and pretentious elegance, could not take this law seriously; while it was the duty of Tiberius, who always protested by deed as by word against the barren pomp of the rich, to see that his wife serve as an example of simplicity to the other matrons of Rome.

Very soon there occurred an accident, not uncommon in unfortunate marriages, but which for special reasons was, in the family of Tiberius, far more than wontedly dangerous. Tacitus tells us that after Julia was out of favour with Tiberius, she contracted a relation with an elegant young aristocrat, one Sempronius Gracchus, of the family of the famous tribunes. Accepting as true the affirmation of Tacitus, in itself likely, we can very well explain the behaviour and acts of Tiberius in these years. The misdoing of Julia offended not only the man and husband, but placed also the statesman, the representative of the traditionalist party, in the gravest perplexity.

According to the *lex de adulteriis,* made by Augustus in the year 18, the husband ought either to punish the unfaithful wife himself or denounce her to the prætor. Could he, Tiberius, provoke so frightful a scandal in the house of the "First Citizen of the Republic"; drive from Rome, defamed, the daughter of Augustus, the most noted lady of Rome, who had so many friends in all circles of its society? Suetonius speaks of the disgust of Tiberius for Julia, *"quam neque criminari aut demittere auderet"*—whom he dared neither incriminate nor repudiate. On the other hand, did not he, the intransigeant traditionalist, who kept continually reproving the nobility for their laxity in self-discipline, merit rebuke, for allowing this thing to go on, not applying the law? The difficulty was serious; the *lex de adulteriis* began to be a torment to its creators. Unable to separate from, unwilling to live with, this woman who had traduced him and whom he despised, Tiberius was reduced to maintaining a merely apparent union to avoid the scandal of a trial and divorce.

This proceeding, however, was an expedient in that condition of things both insufficient and dangerous. The discord between Tiberius and Julia put into the hands of the young nobility, up to that time unarmed, a terrible weapon against the illustrious general, who was, meanwhile, fighting the Germans. The young nobility, inimical to the social laws and to Tiberius, rallied about Julia, and the effects of this alliance were not slow in appearing. Julia had had five sons by Agrippa, of whom the eldest two, Caius and Lucius, had been adopted by Augustus. In the year 6 B.C., the eldest, Caius, reached the age of fourteen. He was therefore but a lad; notwithstanding his youth, there was suddenly brought forward the strange, almost incredible, proposal to make a law by which he might at once be elected consul for the year 754 A.U.C., when he would be twenty years old.

Who made this proposal? Augustus, if we believe Suetonius, out of excessive fondness for his adopted sons. Dion, on the contrary, tells these things differently. He says that from the beginning Augustus opposed the law, and so leads us to doubt that it was either proposed or desired by that Prince. The facts are that a party in Rome kept insisting till Augustus supported this law with his authority, and that from the first he was unwilling to be accessory to an election that overturned without reason every Roman constitutional right.

Who then were these strange admirers of a child of fourteen, who to make him consul did not hesitate to do violence to tradition, to the laws, to good sense, and, finally, to the adoptive father? It was the opposition to Tiberius, the party of the young nobility and Julia, who were seeking a rule less severe, and, if not the abolition, at least the mitigated application of the great social laws. They aimed to put forward the young Caius, to set him early before public attention, to hasten his political career, in order to oppose a rival to Tiberius; to prepare another collaborator and successor of Augustus, to make Tiberius less indispensable and therefore less powerful.

In brief, here was the hope of using against Tiberius at once the maternal pride and affection of Julia, the tenderness of Augustus, and the popularity of the name of Cæsar, which Caius carried. The people had never greatly loved the name of the Claudii, a haughty line of invincible aristocrats, always hard and overbearing with the poor, always opposed to the democratic party. The party against Tiberius hoped that when to a Claudius there should be opposed a Cæsar, the public spirit would revert to the dazzling splendour of the name.

Now we understand why Augustus had at first objected. The privileges that he had caused to be conceded to Marcellus, to Drusus, to Tiberius, were all of less consequence than those demanded for Caius and had all been justified either by urgent needs of State, or services already rendered; but how could it be tolerated that without any reason, without the slightest necessity, there should be made consul a lad of fourteen, of whom it would be difficult to predict even whether he would become a man of common sense? Moreover Augustus could not so easily bring himself to offend Tiberius, who would not admit that the chief of the

Republic should help his enemies offer him so great an affront. How could it be, that while he, amid fatigues and perils in cold and savage regions, was fighting the Germans and holding in subjection the European provinces, that *jeunesse dorée* of good-for-nothings, cynics, idlers, poets, which infested the new generation, was conniving with his wife to set against him a child of fourteen?—to gain, as it were, sanction from a law that the State would not be safe till by the side of this Claudius should be placed a Cæsar, beardless and inexpert, as if the name of the latter outweighed the genius and experience of the former? And Augustus, the head of the Republic, would he have tolerated such an outrage? Tiberius not only resisted the law but exacted the open disapproval of Augustus; in fact, at the beginning, Augustus stood out against it as Tiberius wished; but difficulties grew by the way and became grave.

Julia and her friends knew how to dispose public opinion ably in their own favour, to intrigue in the Senate, to exploit the increasing unpopularity of the social laws, of the spreading aversion to Tiberius and the admiration for other members of Augustus's family. The proposal to make Caius consul became in a short time so popular for one or another of these reasons, and as the symbol of a future government less severe and traditionalistic, that Augustus felt less and less able to withstand the current. On the other hand, to yield meant mortally to offend Tiberius. Finally, as was his wont, this astute politician thought to extricate himself from the difficulty by a transaction and an expedient. Dion, shortly after having said that Augustus finally yielded to the popular will, adds that, to make Caius more modest, he gave Tiberius the tribunician power for five years and charged him with subduing the revolt in Armenia. Augustus's idea is clear: he was trying to please everybody—the partisans of Caius Cæsar by not opposing the law, and Tiberius, by giving the most splendid compensation, making him his colleague in place of Agrippa.

Unfortunately, Tiberius was not the man to accept this compensation. No honour could make up for the insult Augustus had done him, though yielding but in part to his enemies, because by so doing even Augustus had seemed to think it necessary to set him beside a lad of fourteen; he would go away; they might do as they pleased and charge Caius with directing the war in Germany. Indignant at the timid opportunism of Augustus, disgusted with the wife whom he could neither accuse nor repudiate, Tiberius demanded permission of Augustus to retire to Rodi to private life, saying that he was tired and in need of repose. Naturally Augustus was frightened, begged and pleaded with him to remain, sent his mother Livia to beseech him, but every effort was futile; Tiberius was obstinate, and finally, since Augustus did not permit his departure, he threatened to let himself die of hunger. Augustus still tried to stand firm; one day, two days, three days, he let him fast without giving the required consent. At the end of the fourth day, Augustus had to recognise that Tiberius had serious intent to kill himself, and yielded. The Senate granted him permission to depart; and Tiberius at once started for Ostia, "without saying a word," writes Suetonius, "to those who accompanied him, and kissing but a few."

It would be impossible to decide whether this retaliation of Tiberius's self-love was equal to the offence; and perhaps it is useless to discuss the point. It is certain, however, that the consequences of the departure of Tiberius were weighty. The first result was that the party of the young nobility, the party averse to the laws of the year 18, found itself master of the field; perhaps because the opposing party lost with Tiberius its most authoritative leader; perhaps because Augustus, irritated against Tiberius, inclined still more toward the contrary party; perhaps because public opinion judged severely the departure of Tiberius, who, already little admired, became decidedly unpopular. Julia and her friends triumphed, and not content with having conquered, wished to domineer; shortly afterward they obtained the concession of the same privileges as those granted to Caius for his younger brother Lucius. At the same time, Augustus prepared to make Caius and Lucius his two future collaborators in place of Tiberius; Ovid set his hand to a book still more scandalous and subversive than the *Amores,* the

Ars Amandi; public indulgence covered with its protection all those accused on grounds of the laws of the year 18; and finally, the two boys, Caius and Lucius, became popular, like great personages, all over Italy. There have been found in different cities of the peninsula inscriptions in their honour, one of which, very long and curious, is at Pisa; it is full of absurd eulogies of the two lads, who had as yet done nothing, good or bad. Italy must have been tired enough of a too conservative government, which had lasted twenty-five years, of an Empire reconquered by traditional ideas, if, in order to protest, it lionised the two young sons of Agrippa in ways that contradicted every idea and sentiment of Roman tradition.

In conclusion, the departure of Tiberius, and the severe judgment the public gave it, still further weakened the conservative party, already for some years in decline, by a natural transformation of the public spirit. Perhaps the party of tradition would have been entirely spent, had not events soon reminded Rome that its spirit was the life of the military order. The departure of Tiberius, the man who represented this spirit, rapidly disorganised the army and the external policy of Rome. Up to that time Augustus had had beside him a powerful helper—first Agrippa, afterwards Tiberius; but then he found himself alone at the head of the Empire, a man already well on in years; and for the first time it appeared that this zealous bureaucrat, this fastidious administrator, this intellectual idler, who could do an enormous amount of work on condition that he be not forced to issue from his study and encounter currents of air too strong for him, was insufficient to direct alone the politics of an immense empire, which required, in addition to the sagacity of the administrator and the ingenuity of the legislator, the resoluteness of the warrior and the man of action.

The State rapidly fell into a stupor. In Germany, where it was necessary to proceed to the ordering of the province, everything was suspended; the people, apparently subdued, were not bound to pay any tribute, and were left to govern themselves solely and entirely by their own laws—a strange anomaly in the history of the Roman conquests, which only the departure of Tiberius can explain. At such a distance, when he was no longer counselled by Tiberius who so well understood German affairs, Augustus trusted no other assistants, fearing lack of zeal and intelligence; distrusting himself also, he dared initiate nothing in the conquered province. The Senate, inert as usual, gave it not a thought. So Germany remained an uncertainty, neither a province nor independent, for fifteen years, a fact wherein is perhaps to be found the real cause of the catastrophe of Varus, which ruined the whole German policy of Rome.

Furthermore, in Pannonia and Dalmatia, when it was known that the most valiant general of Rome was in disgrace at Rodi, the malcontents took fresh courage, reopened an agitation that could but terminate in a revolt, much more dangerous than any preceding. In the Orient, Palestine arose in 4 B.C., on the death of Herod the Great, against his son, Archelaus, and against the Hellenised monarchy, demanding to be made a Roman province like Syria, and a frightful civil war illumined with its sinister glare the cradle of Jesus. The governor of Syria, Quintilius Varus, threw himself into Judea and succeeded in crushing the revolt; but Augustus, unable to bring himself either to give full satisfaction to the Hebrew people or to execute entirely the testament of Herod, decided as usual on a compromise: he divided the ancient kingdom of Herod the Great among three of his sons, and changed Archelaus's title of king to the more modest one of ethnarch. Then new difficulties arose with the Empire of the Parthians. In short, vaguely, in every part of the Empire and beyond its borders, there began to grow the sense that Rome was again weakening; a sense of doubt due to the decadence of the spirit of tradition and of the party representing it; to the new spirit of the new generation; and finally, to the absence of Tiberius, the one capable general of the time, which gradually disorganised even the western armies, the best in the Empire.

This dissolution of the State naturally fed in the traditionalist party the hope of reconquering. Tiberius had sincere friends and admirers, especially among the nobility, less numerous than those of Julia, but more serious, because his merits were real. Many people among the higher classes — even though, like Augustus, they considered the obduracy of Tiberius excessive — thought that Rome no more possessed so many examples of illustrious men as to be able to retire its best general at thirty-seven. Very soon there arose in the circles about Augustus, in the Senate, in the comitia, a bitter contention between Tiberius's friends and his enemies; this was really a struggle between the traditionalist party, which busied itself conserving, together with the traditions of the old Romanism, the military and political power of Rome, and the party of the young nobility, which, without heeding the external dangers, wished to impel habits, ideas, the public spirit, toward the freer, broader forms of the Oriental civilisation, even at the risk of dissolving the State and the army. Julia and Tiberius personify the two parties; between them stands Augustus, who ought to decide, and is more uncertain than ever. Theoretically Augustus always inclined more toward Tiberius, but from disgust at his departure, from solicitude for domestic peace, from his little sympathy with his step-son, he was driven to the opposite party.

In this duel, what was the behaviour and the part of Livia, the mother of Tiberius? The ancient historians tell us nothing; it is, at all events, hardly probable that Livia remained an inactive witness of the long struggle waged to secure the return of Tiberius and his reinstatement in the brilliant position once his. Moreover, Suetonius says that during his entire stay at Rodi, Tiberius communicated with Augustus by means of Livia. At any rate, the party of Tiberius was not long in understanding that he could not re-enter Rome, as long as Julia was popular and most powerful there; that to reopen the gates of Rome to the husband, it was necessary to drive out the wife. This was a difficult enterprise, because Julia was upheld by the party already dominant; she had the affection of Augustus; she was the mother of Caius and Lucius Cæsar, the two hopes of the Republic, whose popularity covered her with a respect and a sympathy that made her almost invulnerable. Tiberius, instead, was unpopular. However, there is no undertaking impossible to party hate. Exasperated by the growing disfavour of public opinion, the party of Tiberius decided on a desperate expedient to which Tiberius himself would not have dared set hand; that is, since Julia had a paramour, to adopt against her the weapon supplied by the *lex Julia de adulteriis,* made by her father, and so provoke the terrible scandal that until then every one had avoided in fear.

Unfortunately, we possess too few documents to write in detail the history of this dreadful episode; but everything becomes clear enough if one sees in the ruin of Julia a kind of terrible political and judicial blackmailing, tried by the friends of Tiberius to remove the chief obstacle to his return, and if one takes it that the friends of Tiberius succeeded in procuring proofs of the guilt of Julia and carried them to Augustus, not as to the head of the State, but to the father. Dion Cassius says that "Augustus finally, although tardily, came to recognise the misdeeds of his daughter," which signifies that at a given moment, Augustus could no longer feign ignorance of her sins, because the proofs were in the power of irreconcilable enemies, who would have refused to smother the scandal. These mortal enemies of Julia could have been no other than the friends of Tiberius. Julia had violated the law on adultery made by himself; Augustus could doubt it no more.

To understand well the tragic situation in which Augustus was placed by these revelations, one must remember various things: first that the *lex de adulteriis,* proposed by Augustus himself, obliged the father—when the husband could not, or would not—to punish the guilty daughter, or to denounce her to the prætor, if he had not the courage to punish her himself; second, that this law arranged that if the father and the husband failed to fulfil their proper duty, any one whoever, the first comer, might in the name of public morals make the denunciation to the prætor and stand to accuse the woman and her accomplice. Tiberius, the husband, being absent at Rodi, he, Augustus, the father, must become the Nemesis of his daughter—must punish her or denounce her; if not, the friends of Tiberius could accuse her to the prætor, hale her before the quæstor, unveil to the public the shame of her private life.

What should he do? Many a father had disdainfully refused to be the executioner of his own daughter, leaving to others the grim office of applying the *lex Julia*. Could he imitate such an example? He was the head of the Republic, the most powerful man of the Empire, the founder of a new political order; he could decide peace and war, govern the Senate at his pleasure, exalt or abase the powerful of the earth with a nod; and exactly for this reason he dared not evade the bitter task. He feared the envy, the moral and levelling prejudices of the middle classes, which needed every now and then to slaughter in the courts some one belonging to the upper classes, in order to delude themselves that justice is equal for all. To him had been granted the greatest privileges; but precisely on this account was it dangerous to try to cover his daughter with a privileged protection as prey too delicate for public attack. And then, if he himself gave the example of disobeying his law, who would observe it? The tremendous scandal would unnerve all the moral force of his legislation, which was the base of his prestige. The moment was terrible. Imagine this old man of sixty-two wearied by forty-four years of public life, embittered by the difficulties that sprang up about him, disquieted by the dissolution of State of which he was the impotent witness, finding himself all at once facing these alternatives—either destroy his daughter, or undo all the political work over which he had laboured for thirty years; and no temporising possible!

Augustus was not a naturally cruel man, but before these alternatives his mind seems to have been for a moment convulsed by an access of grief and rage, the distant echo of which has come down to us. One moment, as Suetonius says, he had the idea of killing Julia. Then reason, pity, affection, gentler habits, prevailed. He did not give the sentence of death, but he was too practised a politician not to understand that she could not be saved; and as he had immolated Cicero, Lepidus, Antony, so he immolated her also to the necessity of preserving before Italy his prestige of severe legislator and impartial magistrate. To avoid the trial, he resolved to punish her himself with his power of *pater familias* according to the *lex Julia,* exiling her to Pandalaria and announcing the divorce to her in the name of Tiberius. He then despatched to the Senate a record of what he had done, and went away to the country, where he remained a long time, says Suetonius, seeing no one, the prey to profound grief.

It seems that Julia's fall was a surprise to the public. In a day it learned that the highly popular daughter of Augustus had been condemned to exile by her father. This unexpected revelation let a storm loose in the metropolis. Even though there were not then published in Rome those vile newspapers, the pests of modern civilisation, that hunt their *soldi* in the mud and slime of the basest human passions, the taste for scandalous revelations, the envy of genius and fortune, the pleasure of wreaking cruelty upon the unarmed, the low delight in pouring the basest feelings upon the honour of a woman abandoned by all—these passions animated minds then, as they do to-day; nor were there then wanting, more than now, wretches that profited by them, to gather money or satisfy bad instincts, without being able to dispose of a single, miserable sheet of paper. On every side delators sprang up, and an epidemic of slanders embittered Rome; every man who had name or wealth or some relation with the family of Augustus, ran the risk of being accused as a lover of Julia. Several youths of high society, frightened by these charges, committed suicide; others were condemned. About Julia were invented and spread the most atrocious calumnies, which formed thereafter the basis for the infamous legends that have remained in history attached to her name. The traditionalist party naturally abetted this furor of accusations and inventions, made to persuade the public that a fearful corruption was hidden among the upper classes and that to cure it fire and sword must be used without pity.

The friends of Julia, the party of the young nobility, discon-certed at first by the explosion, did not delay to collect themselves and react; the populace of Rome made some great demonstra-tions in favour of Julia and demanded her pardon of Augustus. Many indeed, recognising that her punishment was legal, protested against the ferocity of her enemies, who had not hesi-tated to embitter with so terrible a scandal the old age of Augustus; protested against the mad folly of incrimination with which every part of Rome was possessed. Most people turned, the more envenomed, against Tiberius, attacking him with renewed fury as the cause of all the evil. He it was, they insisted, who had conceived the abominable scandal, willed it, imposed it upon Rome and the Empire!

If Livia and the friends of Tiberius had thought to bring him in by the gate where Julia went out, they were not slow in recognising themselves deceived. The fall of Julia struck Tiberius on the rebound in his distant island. His unpopularity, already great, grew by all the disgust that the scandal about Julia had provoked, and became so formidable that one day about this time the inhabitants of Nimes overturned his statues. It was the beginning of the Christian era, but a dark silence brooded over the Palatine; the defamed Julia was making her hard way to Pandalaria; Tiberius, discredited and detested, was wasting himself in inaction at Rodi; Augustus in his empty house, disgusted, distrustful, half paralysed by deep grief, would hear to no counsels of peace, of indulgence, of reconciliation. Tiberius and Julia were equally hateful to him, and as he did not allow himself to be moved by the friends of Julia, who did not cease to implore her pardon, so he resisted the friends of Tiberius, who tried to persuade him to reconciliation. What mattered it to him if the administration of the State fell to pieces on all sides; if Germans threatened revolt; if Rome had need of the courage, of the valour, of the experience of Tiberius?

Tiberius from his retreat in Rodi kept every one in Rome afraid, beginning with Augustus. Too rich, too eager now for pleasures and comforts, Rome was almost disgusted with the virtues and the defects that had in fact created it, and which survived in Tiberius—aristocratic pride, the spirit of rigour in authority, military valour, simplicity. Peace had come, extending everywhere, with wealth, the desire for enjoyment, happiness, pleasure, freedom, loosening everywhere the firmest bonds of social discipline, persuading Rome to lay down the heavy armour it had worn for so many centuries.

In this family quarrel, which comprises a struggle of everlasting tendencies, Julia represented the new spirit that will prevail, Tiberius, the old, destined to perish; but for the time being, both spirits, however opposed, were necessary; for peace did not expand its gifts in the Empire without the protection of the great armies that fought on the Rhine and on the Danube. If the spirit of peace refreshed Rome, Italy, the Provinces, only the old aristocratic and military spirit could keep the Germans on the Rhine. As in all great social conflicts, the two opposing parties were both, in a certain measure and each from its own point of view, right. Just for that reason, the equilibrium could be found only by a continual struggle in which men on one side and on the other were destined in turn to triumph or fall according to the moment; a struggle in which Augustus, fated to act the part of judge—that is, to recognise, with a final formal sanction, a sentence already pronounced by facts—had against his will in turn to condemn some and reward others.

Julia will remain at Pandalaria, and Tiberius will return to Rome when the danger on the Rhine becomes too threatening, yet without much lessening the conclusive vengeance of Julia. That will come in the long torment of the reign of Tiberius; in the infamy that will pursue him to posterity. After having been pitilessly hated and persecuted in life, this man and this woman, who had personified two social forces eternally at war with each other, will both fall in death into the same abyss of unmerited infamy: tragic spectacle and warning lesson on the vanity of human judgments!

WINE IN ROMAN HISTORY

In history as it is generally written, there are to be seen only great personages and events, kings, emperors, generals, ministers, wars, revolutions, treaties. When one closes a huge volume of history, one knows why this state made a great war upon that; understands the political thinking, the strategic plans, the diplomatic agreements of the powerful, but would hardly be able to answer much more simple questions: how people ate and drank, how the warriors, politicians, diplomats, were clad, and in general how men lived at any particular time.

History does not usually busy itself with little men and small facts, and is therefore often obscure, unprecise, vague, tiresome. I believe that if some day I deserve praise, it will be because I have tried to show that everything has value and importance; that all phenomena interweave, act, and react upon each other — economic changes and political revolutions, costumes, ideas, the family and the state, land-holding and cultivation. There are no insignificant events in history; for the great events, like revolutions and wars, are inevitably and indissolubly accompanied by an infinite number of slight changes, appearing in every part of a nation: if in life there are men without note, and if these make up the great majority of nations — that which is called the "mass" — there is no greater mistake than to believe they are extraneous to history, mere inert instruments in the hands of the oligarchies that govern. States and institutions rest on this nameless mass, as a building rests upon its foundations.

I mean to show you now by a typical case the possible importance of these little facts, so neglected in history. I shall speak to you neither of proconsuls nor of emperors, neither of great conquests nor of famous laws, but of wine-dealers and vine-tenders, of the fortuned and famous plant that from wooded mountain-slopes, mirrored in the Black Sea, began its slow, triumphal spread around the globe to its twentieth century bivouac, California. I shall show you how the branches and tendrils of the plant of Bacchus are entwined about the history and the destiny of Rome.

For many centuries the Romans were waterdrinkers. Little wine was made in Italy, and that of inferior quality: commonly not even the rich were wont to drink it daily; many used it only as medicine during illness; women were never to take it. For a long time, any woman in Rome who used wine inspired a sense of repulsion, like that excited in Europe up to a short time ago by any woman who smoked. At the time of Polybius, that is, toward the middle of the second century B.C., ladies were allowed to drink only a little *passum*, — a kind of sweet wine, or syrup, made of raisins, About the women too much given to the beverage of Dionysos, there were terrifying stories told. It was said, for instance, that Egnatius Mecenius beat his wife to death, because she secretly drank wine; and that Romulus absolved him. (Pliny, *Nat. Hist.*, bk. 14, ch. 13). It was told, on the word of Fabius Pictor, who mentioned it in his annals, that a Roman lady was condemned by the family tribunal to die of hunger, because she had stolen from her husband the keys of the wine-cellar. It was said the Greek judge Dionysius condemned to the loss of her dower a wife who, unknown to her husband, had drunk more than was good for her health: this story is one which shows that women began to be allowed the use of wine as a medicine. It was for a long time the vaunt of a true Roman to despise fine wines. For example, ancient historians tell of Cato that, when he returned in triumph from his proconsulship in Spain, he boasted of having drunk on the voyage the same wine as his rowers; which certainly was not, as we should say now, either Bordeaux or Champagne!

Cato, it is true, was a queer fellow, who pleased himself by throwing in the face of the young nobility's incipient luxury a piece of almost brutal rudeness; but he exaggerated, not falsified, the ideas and the sentiments of Romanism. At that time, it was a thing unworthy of a Roman to be a practised admirer of fine wines and to show too great a propensity for them. Then not only was the vine little and ill cultivated in Italy, but that country almost refused to admit its ability to make fine wines with its grapes. As wines of luxury, only the Greek were then accredited and esteemed—and paid for, like French wines to-day; but, though admiring and paying well for them, the Romans, still diffident and saving, made very spare use of them. Lucullus, the famous conqueror of the Pontus, told how in his father's house—in the house, therefore, of a noble family—Greek wine was never served more than once, even at the most elegant dinners. Moreover, this must have been a common custom, because Pliny says, speaking of the beginning of the last century of the Republic, "Tanta vero vino græco gratia erat ut singulæ potiones in convitu darentur"; that is, translating literally, "Greek wine was so prized that only single potions of it were given at a meal." You understand at once the significance of this phrase; Greek wine was served as to-day—at least on European tables—Champagne is served; it was too expensive to give in quantity.

This condition of things began to change after Rome became a world power, went outside of Italy, interfered in the great affairs of the Mediterranean, and came into more immediate contact with Greece and the Orient. By a strange law of correlation, as the Roman Empire spread about the Mediterranean, the vineyard spread in Italy; gradually, as the world politics of Rome triumphed in Asia and Africa, the grape harvest grew more abundant in Italy, the consumption of wine increased, the quality was refined. The bond between the two phenomena— the progress of conquest and the progress of vine-growing—is not accidental, but organic, essential, intimate. As, little by little, the policy of expansion grew, wealth and culture increased in Rome; the spirit of tradition and of simplicity weakened; luxury spread, and with it the appetite for sensations, including that of the taste for intoxicating beverages.

We have but to notice what happens about us in the modern world—when industry gains and wealth increases and cities grow, men drink more eagerly and riotously inebriating beverages—to understand what happened in Italy and in Rome, as gradually wars, tribute, blackmailing politics, pitiless usury, carried into the peninsula the spoils of the Mediterranean world, riches of the most numerous and varied forms. The old-time aversion to wine diminished; men and women, city-dwellers and countrymen, learned to drink it. The cities, particularly Rome, no longer confined themselves to slaking their thirst at the fountains; as the demand and the price for wine increased, the land-owners in Italy grew interested in offering the cup of Bacchus, and as they had invested capital in vineyards, they were drawn on by the same interest to excite ever the more the eagerness for wine among the multitude, and to perfect grape-culture and increase the crop, in imitation of the Greeks. The wars and military expeditions to the Orient not only carried many Italians, peasants and proprietors, into the midst of the most celebrated vineyards of the world, but also transported into Italy slaves and numerous Greek and Asiatic peasants who knew the best methods of cultivating the vine, and of making wines like the Greek, just as the peasants of Piedmont, of the *Veneto,* and of Sicily, have in the last twenty years developed grape-culture in Tunis and California.

Pliny, who is so rich in valuable information on the agricultural and social advances of Italy, tells us that it opened its hills and plains to the triumphal entrance of Dionysus between 130 and 120 B.C., about the time that Rome entered into possession of the kingdom of Pergamus, the largest and richest part of Asia Minor, left to it by bequest of Attalus. Thenceforward, for a century and a half, the progress of grape-growing continued without interruption; every generation poured forth new capital to enlarge the inheritance of vineyards already grown and to plant new ones. As the crop increased, the effort was redoubled to widen the sale, to entice a greater number of people to drink, to put the Italian wines by the side of the Greek.

At the distance of centuries, these vine-growing interests do not appear even in history; but they actually were a most important factor in the Roman policy, a force that helps us explain several main facts in the history of Rome. For example, vineyards were one of the foundations of the imperial authority in Italy. That political form which was called with Augustus the principality, and from which was evolved the monarchy, would not have been founded if in the last century of the Republic all Italy had not been covered with vineyards and olive orchards. The affirmation, put just so, may seem strange and paradoxical, but the truth of it will be easy to prove.

The imperial authority was gradually consolidated, because, beginning with Augustus, it succeeded in pacifying Italy after a century of commotion and civil wars and of foreign invasions, to which the secular institutions of the Republic had not known how to oppose sufficient defence; so that, little by little, right or wrong, the authority of the *Princeps*, as supreme magistrate, and the power of the Julian-Claudian house, which the supreme magistrate had organised, seemed to the Italian multitude the stable foundation of peace and order. But why was Italy, beginning with the time of Cæsar, so desperately anxious for peace and order? It would be a mistake to see in this anxiety only the natural desire of a nation, worn by anarchy, for the conditions necessary to a common social existence. The contrast of two episodes will show you that during the age of Cæsar annoyance at disorder and intolerance of it had for a special reason increased in Italy. Toward the end of the third century B.C., Italy had borne on its soil for about seventeen years the presence of an army that went sacking and burning everywhere — the army of Hannibal — without losing composure, awaiting with patience the hour for torment to cease. A century and a half later, a Thracian slave, escaping from the chain-gang with some companions, overran the country,—and Italy was frightened, implored help, stretched out its arms to Rome more despairingly than it had ever done in all the years of Hannibal.

What made Italy so fearful? Because in the time of Hannibal it had chiefly cultivated cereals and pastured cattle, while in the days of Spartacus a considerable part of its fortune was invested in vineyards and olive groves. In pastoral and grain regions the invasion of an army does relatively little damage; for the cattle can be driven in advance of the invader, and if grain fields are burned, the harvest of a year is lost but the capital is not destroyed. If, instead, an army cuts and burns olive orchards and vineyards, which are many years in growing, it destroys an immense accumulated capital. Spartacus was not a new Hannibal, he was something much more dangerous; he was a new species of *Phylloxera* or of *Mosca olearia* in the form of brigand bands that destroyed vines and olives, the accumulated capital of centuries. Whence, the emperor became gradually a tutelary deity of the vine and the olive, the fortune of Italy. It was he who stopped the barbarians still restless and turbulent on the frontiers of Italy, hardly over the borders; it was he who kept peace within the country between social orders and political parties; it was he who looked after the maintenance and guarding of the great highways of the peninsula, periodically clearing them of robbers and the evil-disposed that infested them; and the land-owners, who held their vineyards and olive groves more at heart than they did the great republican traditions, placed the image of the Emperor among those of their Lares, and venerated him as they had earlier revered the Senate.

Still more curious is the influence that this development of Italian viticulture exercised on the political life of Rome; for example, in the barbarous provinces of Europe, wine was an instrument of Romanisation, the effectiveness of which has been too much disregarded. In Gaul, in Spain, in Helvetia, in the Danube provinces, Rome taught many things: law, war, construction of roads and cities, the Latin language and literature, the literature and art of Greece; more, it also taught to drink wine. Whoever has read the *Commentaries* of Cæsar will recall that, on several occasions, he describes certain more barbarous peoples of Gaul as prohibiting the importation of wine because they feared they would unnerve and corrupt themselves by habitual drunkenness. Strabo tells us of a great Gaeto-Thracian empire that a Gaetic warrior, Borebiste by name, founded in the time of Augustus beyond the Danube, opposite Roman possessions; while this chieftain sought to take from Greek and Latin civilisation many useful things, he severely prohibited the importation of wine. This fact and others similiar, which might be cited, show that these primitive folk, exactly like the Romans of more ancient times, feared the beverage which so easily intoxicates, exactly as in China all wise people have always feared opium as a national scourge, and so many in France would to-day prohibit the manufacture of absinthe.

This hesitation and fear disappeared among the Gauls, after their country was annexed to the Empire; disappeared or was weakened among all the other peoples of the Danube and Rhine regions, and even in Germany, when they fell under Roman dominion; even also while they preserved independence, as little by little the Roman influence intensified in strength. By example, with the merchants, in literature, Rome poured out everywhere the ruddy and perfumed drink of Dionysos, and drove to the wilds and the villages, remote and poor, the national mead — the beverage of fermented barley akin to modern beer.

The Italian proprietors who were enlarging their vineyards — especially those of the valley of the Po, where already at the time of Strabo the grape-crop was very abundant — soon learned that beyond the Alps lived numerous customers. Under Augustus, Arles was already a large market for wines, both Greek and Italian; during the same period, there passed through Aquileia and Leibach considerable trade in Italian wine with the Danube regions. In the Roman castles along the Rhine, among the multitudes of Italians who followed the armies, there was not wanting the wine-dealer who sought with his liquor to infuse into the torpid blood of the barbarian a ray of southern warmth. Everywhere the Roman influence conquered national traditions; wine reigned on the tables of the rich as the lordly beverage, and the more the Gauls, the Pannonians, the Dalmatians, drank, the more money Italian proprietors made from their vineyards.

I have said that Rome diffused at once its wine and its literature: it also diffused its wine through its literature, a fact upon which I should like to dwell a moment, since it is odd and interesting for diverse reasons. We always make a mistake in judging the great literary works of the past. Two or three centuries after they were written, they serve only to bring a certain delight to the mind; consequently, we take for granted they were written only to bring us this delight. On the contrary, almost all literary works, even the greatest, had at first quite another office; they served to spread or to counteract among the author's contemporaries certain ideas and sentiments that the interests of certain directing forces favoured or opposed; indeed very often the authors were admired and remunerated far more for these services rendered to their contemporaries than for the lofty beauty of the literary works themselves.

This is the case with the odes of Horace. To understand all that they meant to say to contemporaries, one must imagine Roman society as it was then, hardly out of a century of conquests and revolutions, in disorder, unbalanced, and still crude, notwithstanding the luxuries and refinements superficially imitated from the Orient; a society eager to enjoy, yet still ill educated to exercise upon itself that discipline of good taste, without which civilisation and its pleasures aggravate more than restrain the innate brutality of men. During the first period of peace, arrived after so great disturbance, that poetry so perfect in form, which analysed and described all the most exquisite delights of sense and soul, infused a new spirit of refinement into habits, and co-operated with laborious education in teaching even the stern conquerors of the world to enjoy all the pleasures of civilisation, alike literature and love, the luxury of the city and the restfulness of the villa, fraternal friendship and good cookery. It taught, too—this master poetry of the senses—to enjoy wine, to use the drink of Dionysos not to slake the thirst, but to colour, with an intoxication now soft, now strong, the most diverse emotions: the sadness of memories, the tendernesses of friendship, the transports of love, the warmth of the quiet house, when without the furious storm and the bitter cold stiffen the universe of nature.

In the poetry of Horace, therefore, wine appears as a pro-teiform god, which penetrates not only the tissues of the body but also the inmost recesses of the mind and aids it in its every contingency, sad or gay. Wine consoles in ill fortune (i., 7), suffuses the senses with universal oblivion, frees from anxiety and the weariness of care, fills the empty hours, and warms away the chill of winter (i., 9). But the wine that has the power to infuse gentle forgetfulness into the veins, has also the contrasting power of rousing lyric fervour in the spirit, the fervour heroic, divining, mystic (iii., 2). Finally, wine is also a source of power and heroism, as well as of joy and sensuous delight; a principle of civilisation and of progress (ii., 14).

I wish I could repeat to you all the Dionysic verse of this old poet from Venosa, whose subjects and motives, even though expressed in the choicest forms, may seem common and conventional in our time and to us, among whom for centuries the custom of drinking wine daily with meals has been a general habit. But these poems had a very different significance when they were written, in that society in which many did not dare drink wine commonly, considering it as a medicine, or as a beverage injurious to the health, or as a luxury dangerous to morals and the purse; in that time when entire nations, like Gaul, hesitated between the invitations of the ruddy vine-crowned Bacchus, come with his legions victorious, and the desperate supplications of Cervisia, the national mead, pale and fleeing to the forests. In those times and among those men, Horace with his dithyrambics affected not only the spirit but the will, uniting the subtle suggestion of his verses to all the other incentives and solicitations that on every side were persuading men to drink. He corroded the ancient Italian traditions, which opposed with such repugnance and so many fears the efforts of the vintners and the vineyard labourers to sell wine at a high price; in this way he rendered service to Italian viticulture.

The books of Horace, while he was still living, became what we might call school text-books; that is, they were read by young students, which must have increased their influence on the mind. Imagine that to-day a great European poet should describe and extol in magnificent verses the sensuous delight of smoking opium; should deify, in a mythology rich in imagery, the inebriating virtues of this product. Imagine that the verses of this poet were read in the schools: you may then by comparison picture to yourself the action of the poems of Horace.

The political and military triumph of Rome in the Mediterranean world signified therefore the world triumph of wine. So true is this, that in Europe and America to-day the sons of Rome drink wine as their national daily beverage. The Anglo-Saxons and Germans drink it in the same way as the Romans of the second century B.C., on formal occasions, or as a medicine. When you see at an European or American table the gold or the ruby of the fair liquor gleaming in the glasses, remember that this is another inheritance from the Roman Empire and an ultimate effect of the victories of Rome; that probably we should drink different beverages if Cæsar had been overcome at Alesia or if Mithridates had been able decisively to reconquer Asia Minor from Rome. It astonishes you to see between politics and enology, between the great historical events and the lot of a humble plant, so close a bond.

I can show you another aspect of this phenomenon, even stranger and more philosophical. I have already said that at the beginning of the first century before Christ, although Italy had already planted many vineyards and gathered generous crops, Italian wines were still little sought after, while the contrary was true of the Greek. Pliny writes:

The wines of Italy were for long despised. . . . Foreign wines had great vogue for some time even after the consulate of Opimius [121 B.C.], and up to the times of our grandfathers, although then Falernian was already discovered.

In the second half of the last century of the Republic and the first half of the first century B.C., this condition of things changed; Italian wines rose to great fame and demand, and took from the Greek the pre-eminence they so long had held. Finally, this pre-eminence formed one of the spoils of world conquest, and that not one of the meagrest. Pliny, writing in the second half of the first century, says (bk. 14, ch. 11):

Among the eighty most celebrated qualities of wine made in all the world, Italy makes about two-thirds; therefore in this it outdoes other peoples.

The first wines that came into note seem to have been those of southern Italy, especially Falernian, and Julius Cæsar seems to have done much to make it known. Pliny tells us (bk. 14, ch. 15) that, in the great popular banquet offered to celebrate his triumph after his return from Egypt, he gave to every group of banqueters a cask of Chian and an *amphore* of Falernian, and that in his third consulate he distributed four kinds of wine to the populace, Lesbian, Chian, Falernian, and Mamertine; two Greek qualities and two Italian. It is evident that he wished officially to recognise national wines as equal to the foreign, in favour of Italian vintners; so that Julius Cæsar, that universal man, has a place not only in the history of the great Italian conquests, but also in that of Italian viticulture.

The wines of the valley of the Po were not long in making place for themselves after those of southern Italy. We know that Augustus drank only Rhetian wine; that is, of the Valtellina, one of the valleys famous also to-day for several delicious wines; we know that Livia drank Istrian wine.

I have said that Italy exported much wine to Gaul, to the Danube regions, and to Germany; to this may be added another remark, both curious and interesting. *The Periplus of the Erytrian Sea,* attributed to Arrianus, a kind of practical manual of geography, compiled in the second century A.D., tells us that in that century Italian wine was exported as far as India; so far had its fame spread! There is no doubt that the wealth in the first and second century A.D., which flowed for every section of Italy, came in part from the flourishing vineyards planted upon its hills and plains; and that the Italians, who had gone to the Orient for reasons political and financial, had fallen upon yet greater fortune in contrabanding Bacchus from the superb vineyards of the Ægean islands, and transporting him to the hills of Italy; a new seat whereon the capricious god of the vine rested for two centuries, until he took again to wandering, and crossed the Alps.

We may at this juncture ask ourselves if this enologic preeminence of Italy was the result only of a greater skill in cultivating the vine and pressing the grapes. I think not. It does not seem that Italy invented new methods of wine-making; it appears, instead, that it restricted itself to imitating what the Greeks had originated. On the other hand, it is certain, at least in northern and central Italy, that, although the vine grows, it does so less spontaneously and prosperously than in the Ægean islands, Greece, and Asia Minor, because the former regions are relatively too cold.

The great fame of the Italian wines had another cause, a political: the world power and prestige of Rome. This psychological phenomenon is found in every age, among all peoples, and is one of the most important and essential in all history. What is beautiful and what is ugly? What is good and what is bad? What is true and what is false? In every period men must so distinguish between things, must adopt or repudiate certain ideas, practise or abandon certain habits, buy certain objects and refuse others; but one should not believe that all peoples make these discernments spontaneously, according to their natural inclination. It always happens that some nations succeed, by war, or money, or culture, in persuading the lesser peoples about them that they are superior; and strong in this admiration, they impose upon their susceptible neighbours, by a kind of continuous suggestion, their own ideas as the truest, their own customs as the noblest, their own arts as the most perfect.

For this reason chiefly, wars have often distant and complicated repercussions on the habits, the ideas, the commerce of nations. War, to which so many philosophers would attribute a divine spirit, so many others a diabolic, appears to the historian as above all a means — allow me the phrase, a bit frivolous, but graphic — of noisy *réclame,* advertisement for a people; because, although a more civilised people may be conquered by one more barbarous, less cultured, less moral; although, also, the superiority in war may be relative, and men are not on the earth merely to give each other blows, but to work, to study, to know, to enjoy; yet the majority of men are easily convinced that he who has won in a war is in everything, or at least in many things, superior to him who has lost. So it happened, for example, after the late Franco-Prussian War, that not only the armies organised or reorganised after 1870 imitated even the German uniform, as they had earlier copied the French, but in politics, science, industry, even in art, everything German was more generously admired. Even the consumption of beer heavily increased in the wine countries, and under the protection of the Treaty of Frankfurt, the god Gambrinus has made some audacious sallies into the territories sacred to Dionysos.

The same thing occurred in regard to wine in the ancient world. Athens and Alexander the Great had given to Greek wine the widest reputation, all the peoples of the Mediterranean world being persuaded that that was the best of all. Then the centre of power shifted to the west, toward the city built on the banks of the Tiber, and little by little as the power of Rome grew, the reputation of its wine increased, while that of Greece declined; until, finally, with world empire, Italy conquered pre-eminence in the wine market, and held it with the Empire; for while Italy was lord, Italian wine seemed most excellent and was paid for accordingly.

This propensity of minor or subject peoples to imitate those dominant or more famous, is the greatest prize that rewards the pre-eminent for the fatigue necessary to conquer that place of honour; it is the reason why cultured and civilised nations ought naturally to seek to preserve a certain political, economic, and military supremacy, without which their intellectual superiority would weaken or at least lose a part of its value. The human multitude in the vast world are not yet so intelligent and refined as to prize that which is beautiful and grand for its own sake; and they are readily induced to admire as excellent what is but mediocre, if behind it there is a force to be feared or to impose it. Indeed, we may observe in the modern world a phenomenon analogous to that in historic Italy. What, in succeeding centuries, have been the changes in the enologic superiority conquered by Rome? Naturally I cannot recount the whole story, although it would be interesting; but will only observe that contemporary civilisation confirms the law by which predominance in the Latin world and the pre-eminence of wine are indissolubly bound together in history.

Paris is the modern Rome, the metropolis of the Latin world. France continues, as far as can be done in modern times, the ancient sway of Rome, irradiating round so much of the globe, by commerce, literature, art, science, industry, dominance of political ideas, the influence of the Latin world, making tributaries to Latin culture of barbarous peoples, and nations too young for leadership or grown too old; and France has inherited the pre-eminence in wines, although it lies at the farthest confines of the vine-bearing zone, beyond which the tree of Bacchus refuses to live. Do you realise that in all the wide belt of earth where vineyards flourish, only the dry hills of Champagne ripen the delicious effervescent wine that refigures in modern civilisation—at least for those who are fond of wine—the nectar of the gods? And this, while effervescent wines are made in innumerable parts of the world and many are so good that one wonders if it were not possible for them, manufactured with care, placed in sightly bottles, and sold at as high a price as the most famous French Champagne, to dispute a part of the admiration that the devotees of Bacchus render to the French wine. Ah, they do not scintillate before the eyes of the world as symbols of gay intoxication like the others, for through those bottles passes no ray of the glory and prestige of France! An historian fond of paradoxes might affirm, and with great likelihood, what does not appear at first glance: that the great brands of French Champagne would not be sold so dear if the French Revolution had been suppressed by the European coalition, and if France, overcome in the terrible trial, had been enchained by the absolute monarchies of Europe like a dangerous beast. It would even be possible to declare that the reputation of Champagne is rooted, not only in the ground where the grapes are cultivated, and preserved in the vast cellars where the precious crops are stored, but in all the historic tradition of France, in all that which has given France worldly glory and power: the victorious wars, the distant conquests, the colonies, the literature, the art, the science, the money capital, and the spirit— cosmopolitan, expansive, dynamic—of its history. It would be possible to declare that it makes and pours into all the world its precious wine by that same virtue, intimate, national, and historic, by which it created the encyclopædia and made the Revolution, let Napoleon loose on Europe and founded the Empire, wrote so many famous books and built on the banks of the Seine the marvellous universal city, where all the forces of modern civilisation are gathered together and hold each other in equilibrium: aristocracy and democracy, the cosmopolite spirit and the spirit of nationality, money and science, war and fashion, art and religion. If France had not had its great history, Champagne would have remained an effervescing wine of modest household use that the peasants place every year in barrels for their own family consumption or to sell in the vicinity of the city of Rheims.

SOCIAL DEVELOPMENT
OF THE ROMAN EMPIRE

AUGUSTUS died the twenty-third of August of the year 14 A.D., saying to Livia, as she embraced him: "Adieu, Livia, remember our
long life." Suetonius adds that, before dying, he had asked the
friends who had come to salute him, if he seemed to them "*mimum
vitæ commode transegisse*"—to have acted well his life's comedy. In
this famous phrase many historians have seen a confession, an
acknowledgment of the long rôle of deceit that the unsurpassable
actor had played to his public. What a mistake! If Augustus did
pronounce that famous sentence, he meant to say quite another
thing. An erudite German has demonstrated with the help of
many texts that the ancient writers, and especially the stoic
philosophers, commonly compared life to a theatrical representa-
tion, divided into different acts and with an inevitable epilogue,
death, without intending to say that it was a thing little serious or
not true. They only meant that life is an action, which has a natural sequence from beginning to end, like a theatrical representa-
tion. There is then no need to translate the expression of
Augustus "the play"—that is, the deceit—"is ended," but rather
"the drama"—the work committed by destiny—"is finished."

The drama was ended, and what a drama! It is difficult to find
in history a longer and more troubled career than that known by
Augustus for nearly sixty years, from the far-away days when,
young, handsome, full of ambition and daring, he had come to
Rome, throwing himself head first into the frightful turmoil let
loose by the murder of Cæsar, to that tranquil death, the death of

a great wise man, in the midst of the *pax Romana,* now spread from end to end of the Empire! After so many tragic catastrophies had struck his class and his family, *Euthanasia*—the death of the happy —descended for the first time since the passing of Lucullus, to close the eyes of a great Roman.

There is no better means of giving an idea of the mission of the Roman Empire in the world than to summarise the life and work of this famous personage. Augustus has been in our century somewhat the victim of Napoleon I. The extraordinary course of events at the beginning of the nineteenth century made so vivid an impression on succeeding generations, that for the whole of the century people have been able to admire only the great agitators, men whose lives are filled with storm and clamorous action. Compared with that of Napoleon or of Cæsar, the figure of Augustus is simple and colourless. The Roman peace, in the midst of which he died, was his work only very indirectly. Augustus had wearied his whole life in reorganising the finances and the army, in crushing the revolts of the European provinces, in defending the boundaries of the Rhine and the Danube, in making effective in Rome, as far as he could, the old aristocratic constitution. All intent on this service, a serious and difficult one, he never dreamed of regenerating the Empire by a powerful administration. Even if he had wished it, he would not have had the means—men and money.

For the past century, the vastness and power of the administration that governed the Empire has been greatly admired. Without discussing many things possible on this point, it must be observed that this judgment does not apply to the times of Augustus and Tiberius, because then this administration did not exist. During the first fifty years of the Empire, the provinces were all governed, as under the Republic, by proconsuls or proprætors, each accompanied by a quæstor, a few subordinate officials, freedmen, friends, and slaves. A few dozen of men governed the provinces, as vast as states. Augustus added to this rudimentary administration but one organ, the procurator, chosen from freedmen or knights, charged with overseeing the collection of tribute and expenses; that is, caring for the interests, not of the provinces, but of Rome. Consequently, the government was weak and inactive in all the provinces.

Whoever fancies the government of Rome modelled after the type of modern governments, invading, omnipotent, omnipresent, deceives himself. There were sent into the provinces nobles belonging to rich and noted families, who had therefore no need to rob the subjects too much; and these men ruled, making use of the laws, customs, institutions, families of nobles, of each place, exactly as England now does in many parts of its Empire. As in general these governors were not possessed of any great activity, they did not meddle much in the internal affairs of the subject peoples. To preserve the unity of the Empire and the supremacy of Italy against all enemies, within and without; to exploit reasonably this supremacy; for the rest, to let every people live as best pleased it: such was the policy of Augustus and of Tiberius, the policy of the first century A.D. In short, this was but the idea of the old aristocratic party, adapted to the new times.

So the Roman Government gave itself little concern at this time for the provinces, nor did it build in them any considerable public work. It did not construct roads, nor canals, nor harbours, except when they were necessary to the metropolis; for example, Agrippa made the network of Gallic roads; Augustus opened the first three great highways that crossed the Alps. It would be a mistake to suppose that these important constructions were designed to favour the progress of Gallic commerce; they were strategic highways made to defend the Rhine. As gradually Gaul grew rich, Rome had to recognise that the weak garrisons, set apart in the year 27 for the defence of the Rhine and the Danube, were insufficient. It would have been necessary to increase the army, but the finances were in bad condition. Augustus then thought to base defence on the principle that the immense frontiers could not all be assailed at the same time, and therefore he constructed some great mili-

tary roads across the Alps and Gaul, to be able to collect the soldiery rapidly from all parts of the Empire at any point menaced,
on the Rhine or on the Danube.

The imperial policy of Augustus and that of Tiberius, who
applied the same principles with still greater vigour, was above all a
negative policy. Accordingly, it could please only those denying as
useful to progress another kind of men, the great agitators of the
masses. Shall we therefore conclude that Augustus and Tiberius
were useless? So doing, we should run the risk of misunderstanding
all the history of the Roman conquest. By merely comprehending
the value of the apparent inactivity of Augustus and Tiberius, one
can understand the essence of the policy of world expansion initiated by the Roman aristocracy after the Second Punic War. At the
beginning, this policy was pre-eminently destructive. Everywhere
Rome either destroyed or weakened, not nations or peoples, but
republics, monarchies, theocracies, principalities—that is, the
political superstructures that framed the different states, great or
small; everywhere it put in place of these superstructures the weak
authority of its governors, of the Senate, of its own prestige; everywhere it left intact or gave greater freedom to the elementary
forms of human association, the family, the tribe, the city.

So for two centuries Rome continued in Orient and Occident
to suppress bureaucracies, to dismiss or reduce armies, to close
royal palaces, to limit the power of priestly castes or republican
oligarchies, substituting for all these complicated organisations
a proconsul with some dozens of vicegerent secretaries and
attendants. The last enterprise of this policy, which I should be
tempted to call "state-devouring," was the destruction of the
dynasty of the Ptolemies, in Egypt. Without doubt, the suppression
of so many states, continued for two centuries, could not be
accomplished without terrible upheavals. It would be useless to
repaint here the grim picture of the last century of the Republic;
sufficient to say, the grandiosity of this convulsion has hindered
most people from seeing that the state-devouring policy of Rome
included in itself, by the side of the forces of dissolution, benefi-

cent, creative forces, able to bring about a new birth. If this policy had not degenerated into an unbridled sacking, it could have effectuated everywhere notable economies in the expenses of government that were borne by the poorer classes, suppressing as it did so many armies, courts, bureaucracies, wars. It is clear that Rome would have been able to gather in on all sides, especially in the Orient, considerable tribute, merely by taking from the various peoples much less than the cost of their preceding monarchies and continuous wars. Moreover, Rome established with the conquests throughout the immense Empire what we would call a régime of free exchange; made neighbours of territories formerly separated by constant wars, unsafe communication, and international anarchy; and rendered possible the opening up of mines and forests hitherto inaccessible.

The apparent inactivity of Augustus and Tiberius was simply the ultimate and most beneficent phase of the state-devouring policy of Rome, that in which, the destructive forces exhausted, the creative forces began to act. Augustus and Tiberius only prolonged indefinitely by means of expedients that mediocre order and that partial tranquillity re-established after Actium by the general weariness; but exactly for this reason were they so useful to the world. In this peace, in this mediocre order, the policy of expansion of Rome, finally rid of all the destructive forces, matured all the benefits inherent within it. Finally, after a frightful crisis, the world was able to enjoy a liberty and an autonomy such as it had never previously enjoyed and which perhaps it will never again in an equal degree of civilisation and in so great an extension.

The Empire then covered Spain, France, Belgium, a part of Germany and Austria, Switzerland and Italy, the Balkanic countries, Greece, Asia Minor, Syria, Palestine, a part of Arabia, Egypt, and all northern Africa. I do not believe that the political *personnel* that made up the central government of this enormous Empire ever comprised more than 2,000 men. The army charged with defending so many territories numbered about 200,000 men — fewer than the present army of Italy alone. The effects of this order of things were soon to be seen; in all the Mediterranean basin there began a rapid and universal economic expansion, which, on a smaller scale, might remind one of what Europe and America have seen in the nineteenth century. New lands were cultivated, new mines opened, new wares manufactured, exports sent into regions formerly closed or unknown; and every new source of wealth, creating new riches, made labour and commerce progress.

Foremost among all nations of the Empire, at the centre, Italy rapidly consolidated its fortune and its domination. After the mad plundering of the times of Cæsar, followed methodical exploiting. Italy attracted to itself by the power of political leadership the precious metals and wares of luxury from every part of the Empire; the largest quantity of these things passed through Rome, before being scattered throughout the peninsula in exchange for the agricultural and industrial products of Italy, consumed in the capital. Consequently the middle classes and many cities grew rich, especially the cities of the Campania, Pompeii, Herculaneum, Naples, Pozzuoli, through which passed all the trade between Italy and Egypt. In addition, Italy found an abundant source of income in the exportation of wine and oil.

In short, having at last emerged from revolution, the peoples of Italy rallied around Rome and the imperial power, united and relatively content. At the same time, the provinces began among themselves, about Italy, a great interchange of merchandise, men, ideas, customs, across the Mediterranean. Rome and Italy were invaded by a crowd of Orientals, slaves, freedmen, merchants, artisans, *litterati*, artists, acrobats, poets, adventurers; and contemporaneously with Rome and Italy, the agricultural provinces of the West, especially those along the Danube. Rome did not conquer the barbarous provinces of Europe for itself alone; it conquered them also for the East, which, in Mesia, Dalmatia, Pannonia, among those barbarians growing civilised and eager to live in cities, found customers for their industries in articles of luxury, for their artists, teachers of literature, and propagandists of religion.

We are therefore able to explain to ourselves why, beginning from the time of Augustus, all the industrial cities of the Orient— Pergamon, Laodicea, Ephesus, Ierapolis, Tyre, Sidon, Alexandria —entered upon an era of new and refulgent prosperity. Finally, we add the singular enriching of two nations, whose names return anew united for the last time, Egypt and Gaul. To all the numerous sources of Gallic wealth there is to be added yet another, the importance of which is easier to understand after what I have said on the development of the Empire. Pliny tells us that all Gaul wove linen sails. The progress of navigation, a consequence of the progress of commerce, much increased the demand for linen sail-cloth, something that explains the spread of flax cultivation in Gaul and the profit derived from it.

As to Egypt, it not only found in the pacified empire new outlets for its old industries, but also succeeded in engaging a large part of the new commerce with the extreme Orient, which was at this time greatly on the increase. From India and China were imported pearls, diamonds, silk fabrics; for the use of these wares gained largely during this century, as it has done in recent times in Europe and America; perfumes were also imported, and rice, which served as a medicament and to prepare dishes of luxury.

The unity of the Empire was due far more to this great economic development that began under Augustus than to the political action of the early emperors. Little by little, imperial interests became so numerous and so considerable that Rome saw the effort necessary to keep up the unity diminish. Everywhere, even in the most distant regions, powerful minorities formed that worked for Rome and against old separating, anti-uniting forces, against old traditions and local patriotism alike. The wealthy classes everywhere became in a special way wholly favourable to Rome. Therefore there is no more serious mistake than regarding the Roman Empire as the exclusive work of a government: it was in truth created by two diverse forces, operating one after the other— each in its own time, for both were necessary: a force of destruction —the state-devouring policy of Rome; a force of reconstruction—

the economic unification. The annihilation of states, without which there would have been no economic unification, was the work of the government and the armies. It was the politicians of the Senate that destroyed so many states by wars and diplomatic intrigues; but the economic unification was made chiefly by the infinitely little—the peasant, the artisan, the educated man—the nameless many, that lived and worked and passed away, leaving hardly trace or record. These unknown that laboured, each seeking his own personal happiness, contributed to create the Empire as much as did the great statesmen and generals. For this reason I can never regard without a certain emotion the mutilated inscriptions in the museums, chance salvage from the great shipwreck of the ancient world, that have preserved the name of some landowner, or merchant, or physician, or freedman. Lo! what remains of these generations of obscure workers, who were the indispensable collaborators of the great statesmen and diplomatists of Rome, and without whom the political world of Rome would have been but a gigantic enterprise of military brigandage!

The great historic merit of Augustus and of Tiberius is that they presided over the passage from the destructive to the reorganising phase with their wise, prudent, apparently inactive policy. The transition, like all transitions, was difficult; the disintegrating forces were not yet exhausted; the upbuilding forces were still very weak; the world of the time was in unstable equilibrium, violent perturbations certainly yet possible. Without doubt, it is hard to say what would have happened if, instead of being governed by the policy of Augustus, the world had fallen into the hands of an adventurous oligarchy like that which gathered around Alexander the Great; but we can at least affirm that the sagacity and prudence of Augustus, which twenty centuries afterward appear as inactivity, did much to avoid such disturbances, the consequences of which, in a world so exhausted, would have been grave.

Nor is it correct to believe that this policy was easy. Moderation and passivity, even when good for the governed, rust and waste away governments, which must always be doing something, even if it be only making mistakes. In fact, while supreme power usually brings return and much return to him who exercises it, especially in monarchies, it cost instead, and unjustly, to Augustus and Tiberius. Augustus had to offer to the monster, as Tiberius called the Empire, almost all his family, beginning with the beloved Julia, and had to spend for the state almost all his fortune. We know that although in the last twenty years of his life he received by many bequests a sum amounting to a billion and four hundred million sesterces, he left his heirs only one hundred and fifty million sesterces, all the rest having been spent by him for the Republic: this was the singular civil list of this curious monarch, who, instead of fleecing his subjects, spent for them almost all he had. It is vain to speak of Tiberius: the Empire cost him the only thing that perhaps he held dear, his fame. A philosophic history would be wrong in not recognising the grandeur of these sacrifices, which are the last glory of the Roman nobility. The old political spirit of the Roman nobility gave to Augustus and Tiberius the strength to make these sacrifices, and they probably saved ancient civilisation from a most difficult crisis.

It may be observed that Augustus and Tiberius worked for the Empire and the future without realising it. Far from understanding that the economic progress of their time would unify the Empire better than could their laws and their legions, they feared it; they believed that it would everywhere diffuse "corruption," even in the armies, and therefore weaken the imperial power of resistance against the barbarians on the Rhine and the Danube. The German peril—the future had luminously to demonstrate it —was much less than Augustus and Tiberius believed. In other words, the first two emperors thought that the unity of the Empire would be maintained by a vigorous, solid army, while the economic progress, which spread "corruption," appeared to them to put it to risk.

Exactly the opposite happened; the army continued to decay, notwithstanding the desperate efforts of Tiberius, while the inner force of economic interests held the countries well bound together. It is impossible to oppose this course of reasoning, in itself most accurate; but what conclusion is to be drawn from it? In the chaotic conflict of passions and interests that make up the world, the deeds of a man or a party are not useful in proportion to the objective truth of the ideas acted out, or to the success attained. Their usefulness depends upon the direction of the effort, on the ends it proposes, on the results it obtains. There are men and parties of whom one might say, they were right to be wrong, when chimerical ideas and mistakes have sustained their courage to carry out an effective effort; there are others, instead, of whom it might be said that they were wrong to be right, when their clear vision of present and past kept them from accomplishing some painful but necessary duty.

Certainly the old Roman traditions were destined to be overwhelmed by the invasion of Oriental ideas and habits; but what might not have happened if every one had understood this from the very times of Augustus; if then no one had opposed the invasion of Orientalism; if mysticism and the monarchy of divine right had transformed Italy or the Empire within fifty years instead of three centuries? I should not at all hesitate to affirm that certain errors are in certain conjunctions much wiser than the corresponding verities. There is nothing more useful in life than resistance, though apparently futile, against social forces fated to perish, because these, struggling on to the very end, always succeed in imposing a part of themselves on the victorious power, and the result is always better than a complete and unantagonised victory of the opposing force. To the obstinate resistance with which republican principles combated Asiatic monarchy in Rome, we must even to-day render thanks for the fact that Europe was not condemned, like Asia, to carry the eternal yoke of semidivine absolutism, even in dynastic régimes. What social force destined to perish would still have power to struggle if it clearly foresaw its inevitable future dissolution; if it did not fortify itself a little with some deluding vision of its own future?

Augustus and Tiberius were deceived. They wished to reanimate what was doomed; they feared what for the moment was not dangerous. They are the last representatives of the policy initiated by the Scipios and not the initiators of the policy that created the bureaucratic Empire of Diocletian: yet this is exactly their glory. They were right to be wrong; and they rendered to the Empire an immense service, for the very reason that the definite outcome of their efforts was diametrically opposed to the idea that animated them. But we need not dwell on this point. Such were the ideas of the two emperors and the results of their work; the true Empire, known to all, the monarchic, Asiaticised, bureaucratic Empire, grew out of this little-governed beginning that Augustus and Tiberius allowed to live in the freedom of the largest autonomy. How was it formed? This is the great problem that I shall try to solve in the sequence of my work. Naturally, I cannot now résumé all the ideas I mean to develop: I confine myself here to some of the simplest considerations, which seem to me surest.

The picture of the Empire, so brilliant from the economic stand-point, is much less so from the intellectual: here we touch its great weakness. Destroying so many governments, especially in the Orient, Rome had at the same time decapitated the intellectual *élites* of the ancient world; for the courts of the monarchies were the great firesides of mental activity. Rome had therefore, together with states and governments, destroyed scientific and literary institutions, centres of art, traditions of refinement, of taste, of æsthetic elegance. So everywhere, with the Roman domination, the practical spirit won above the philosophical and scientific, commerce over arts and letters, the middle classes over historic aristocracies. Already weakened by the overthrow of the most powerful Asiatic monarchies, these *élites* received the final blow on the disappearance of their last protection, the dynasty of the Ptolemies in Egypt.

When Augustus began to govern the Empire, the classes that represent tradition, culture, the elevated and disinterested activities of the spirit, were everywhere extensive in number, in wealth, in energy. It was not long before these ultimate remainders vanished under the alluvial overflow of the middle classes, swollen by the big economic gains of the first century. In this respect, the first and second centuries of the Christian era resemble our own time. In the whole Empire, alike in Rome, in Gaul, in Asia, there were old aristocratic families, rich and illustrious, but they were not the class of greatest power. Under them stood a middle class of merchants, land-owners, orators, jurists, professors, and other intellectual men, and this was so numerous, comfortable, and so potent as to cause all the great social forces, from government to industry, to abandon the old aristocracy and court it like a new mistress. Art, industry, literature, were vulgarised in those two centuries, as to-day in Europe and America, because they had to work mainly for this middle class which was much more numerous, and yet cruder than the ancient *élites*. It was the first era of the *cheap*, of vulgarisations, I was about to say of the *made in Germany*, that enters into history. There was invented the art of silver-plating, to give the *bourgeoisie* at moderate prices the sweet illusion of possessing objects of silver; great thinkers disappeared; instead were multiplied manuals, treatises, encyclopædias, professors that summarised and vulgarised. Philosophy gradually gave out, like all the higher forms of literature, and there began the reign of the declaimers and the sophists; that is, the lecture-givers, the lawyers, the journalists. In painting and sculpture, original schools were no more to be found, nor great names, but the number of statues and bas-reliefs increased infinitely. The paintings of Pompeii and many statues and marbles that are now admired in European museums are examples of this industrialised art, inexpensive, creating nothing original, but furnishing to families in comfortable circumstances passable copies of works of art—once a privilege only of kings.

The imperial bureaucracy that was formed mainly in the second century was another effect of this enlargement of the middle classes. In the second century there came into vogue many humanitarian ideas, which have a certain resemblance to modern ones.

There increased solicitude for the general well-being, for order, for justice, and this augmented the number of functionaries charged with insuring universal felicity by administrative means. The movement was supported by intellectual men of the middle classes, especially by jurists, who sought to put their studies to profit, getting from the government employments in which they might make use, well or ill, of their somewhat artificial aptitudes. If the aristocratic idea, personified by Augustus and Tiberius, delayed, it could not stop, the invasion of these bureaucratic locusts; the government showed itself constantly weaker with the intellectual classes. Little by little the whole Empire was bureaucratised; founded by an aristocracy exclusively Roman in statesmen and soldiers, it was finally governed by a cosmopolitan bureaucracy of men of brains: orators, *litterati,* lawyers. Therefore, to my thinking, they are wrong who believe that the imperial bureaucracy created the unity of the Empire; whereas, the formation of the imperial bureaucracy was one of the consequences of that natural unification, the chief reason for which should be sought in the great economic movement. The economic unification was first and was entire; then came the political unity, made by the imperial bureaucracy, which was less complete than the unifying of material interests.

After the material unity, after the political, there should have been formed the moral and intellectual; but at this point, the forces of Rome gave way. Rome had gathered under its sceptre too many races, too many kinds of culture, religions too diverse; its spirit was too exclusively political, administrative, and judicial; it could not therefore conciliate the ideas, assimilate the customs, weld the sentiments, unify the religions, by its laws and decrees. To this end was necessary the power of ideas, of doctrines, of beliefs that officials of administration could neither create nor propagate. The work was to be accomplished outside of, and in part against, the government. It is the work of Christianity.

Many have asked me how I shall consider Christianity in the sequence of my work. In brief, I may say that I shall follow a different method from that which its historians have taken up to this time: they have studied especially how there was formed that part of Christianity which yet lives and is the soul of it, namely, the religious doctrine. On this account, they generally separate its history from the history of the Empire, making of it the principal argument, considering the history of Roman society as subordinate to it and therefore only an appendix. I propose to reverse the study, taking Christianity as a chapter, important but separate, in the history of the Empire. If for three centuries Christianity has been gradually returning to its origin, that is, becoming purely a religion and a moral teaching, for some centuries in the ancient world it was a thing much more complicated; a government and an administration that willed not only to regulate the relations between man and God, but to govern the intellectual, social, moral, political, and economic life of the people. The historian ought to explain how this new Empire—for it was indeed a new Empire—was formed in Rome and upon its ruins: this is a problem much more intricate than at first appears.

It has been said and often repeated that the Church was in the Middle Ages in Europe the continuation of the Roman Empire, that the Pope is yet the real successor of the Emperor in Rome. In fact he carries one of the Emperor's titles, *Pontifex maximus*. The observation is just, but it should not make us forget that the Christian Empire, so to call it, and the Roman Empire were between themselves as radically opposed as two forces that created the one and the other: politics and intellectuality. The diplomatists, the generals, the legislators of Rome created by political means, by wars, treaties, laws, a grand economic and political unity, which they consolidated, quite giving up the formation of a large intellectual and moral unity. The intellectual men, who formed the most powerful nucleus of the Church after the fourth century, took up again the Roman idea of unity and of empire; but they transferred it from matter to mind, from the concrete world of economic and political interests, to the world of ideas and beliefs. They tried to re-do, by pen and word, the work of the Scipios, of Lucullus, and of Cæsar, to conquer the world, not indeed invading it with armies, but spreading a new faith, creating a new morality, a new metaphysics which must gather up within themselves the intellectual activities of Græco-Latin culture, from history to science, from law to philosophy.

The Church of the Middle Ages was therefore the most splendid edifice that the intellectual classes have so far created. The power of this empire of men of letters increased, as little by little the other empire, that of the generals and diplomats, declined. Christianity saw with indifference the Roman Empire decay; indeed, when it could, it helped on the disintegration and was one of the causes of that political and economic pulverising which everywhere succeeded the great Roman unity. Political and economic unity on the one hand, moral and intellectual on the other, seem in the history of European civilisation things opposite and irreconcilable; when one is formed, the other is undone. As the Roman Empire had found in intellectual and moral disunion a means of preserving more easily the economic and political unity, the Church broke to pieces the political and economic unity of the ancient world to make, and for a long time preserve, its own moral and intellectual oneness.

I shall make an effort, above all, to explain the origin, the development, and the consequences of this contradiction, because I believe that explaining this clears one of the weightiest and most important points in all the history of our civilisation; in truth, this contradiction seems to be the immortal soul of it. For instance: in time, Augustus is twenty centuries away from us, but mentally and morally he is, instead, much nearer, because for the last four centuries Europe has been returning to Rome—that is, striving to remake a great political and economic unity at the expense of the intellectual and moral. In this fact particularly, lies the immense historic importance of what is called the classic renaissance. It indicates the beginning of an historic reversion that corresponds in the opposite direction to what occurred in the third and fourth centuries of the Christian era. The classic renaissance freed anew the scientific spirit of the ancients from mediæval metaphysics and therefore created the sciences; rediscovered some basic political and juridical ideas of the ancient world, among them that of the indivisibility of the State, which destroyed the foundations of feudalism and of all the political orders of the Middle Ages; and gave a great impetus to the struggle against the political domination of the Church and toward the formation of the great states. France and England have been in the lead, and for two centuries Europe has been wearying itself imitating them.

After the movement of political unification followed the economic. Look about you: what do you see? A world that looks more like the Roman Empire than it does the Middle Ages; it is a world of great states whose dominating classes have almost all the essential ideas of Græco-Latin civilisation; each, seeking to better its own conditions, is forced to establish between itself and the others the strictest economic relations and to bind into the system of common interests also barbarous countries and those of differing civilisation. But how? By scrupulously respecting all the intellectual and moral diversities of men. What matters it if a people be Roman Catholic or Protestant, Mohammedan or Buddhist, monarchic or republican, provided it buys, sells, takes part in the economic unity of the modern world? This is the policy of contemporary states and was the policy of the Roman Empire. It has often been observed that in the modern world, so well administered, there is an intellectual and moral diversity greater than that during the fearful anarchy of the Middle Ages, when all the lettered classes had a single language, the Latin, and the lower classes held, on certain fundamental questions, the same ideas—those taught by the Church. A correct observation, this, but one from which there is no need to draw too many conclusions; since in our history the material unity and the ideal are naturally exclusive.

We are returning, in a vaster world, to the condition of the Roman Empire at its beginning; to an immense economic unity, which, notwithstanding the aberrations of protectionism, is grander and firmer than all its predecessors; to a political unity not so great, yet considerable, because even if peace be not eternal, it is at least the normal condition of the European states; to an indifference for every effort put forth to establish moral and ideal uniformity among the nations, great and small, that share in this political and economic unity. This is why we understand Augustus and his times much more readily than we do the times of Charlemagne, even though from the latter we possess a greater number of documents; this is why we can write a history of Augustus and rectify so many mistakes made about him by preceding generations. It has often happened to me to find, *à propos* of the volumes written on Augustus, that my contradiction of tradition creates a kind of instinctive diffidence. Many say: "Yes, this book is interesting; but is it possible that for twenty centuries everybody has been mistaken? — that it was necessary to wait till 1908 to understand what occurred in the year 8?" But those twenty centuries reduce themselves, as far as regards the possibility of understanding Augustus, to little more than a hundred years. Since Augustus was the last representative of a world that was disappearing, his figure soon became obscure and enigmatic. Tacitus and Suetonius saw him already enveloped in the mist of that new spirit which for so many centuries was to conceal from human eyes the wonderful spectacle of the pagan world. Then the mist became a fog and grew denser, until Augustus disappeared, or was but a formless shadow. Centuries passed by; the fog began to withdraw before the returning sun of the ancient culture; his figure reappeared. Fifty years ago, the obscurity cleared quite away; the figure stands in plain view with outlines well defined. I believe that the history I have written is more like the truth than those preceding it, but I do not consider myself on that account a wonder-worker. I know I have been able to correct many preceding errors, because I was the first to look attentively when the moment to see and understand arrived.

ROMAN HISTORY IN
MODERN EDUCATION

WHEN I announced my intention to write a new history of Rome, many people manifested a sense of astonishment similar to what they would have felt had I said that I meant to retire to a monastery. Was it to be believed that the hurrying modern age, which bends all its energies toward the future, would find time to look back, even for a moment, at that past so far away? That my attempt was rash was the common opinion not only of friends and critics, but also of publishers, who everywhere at first showed themselves skeptical and hesitating. They all said that the public was quite out of touch with Roman affairs. On the contrary, facts have demonstrated that also in this age, in aspect so eager for things modern, people of culture are willing to give attention to the events and personages of ancient Rome.

The thing appears strange and bizarre, as is natural, to those who had not considered it possible; consequently, few have seen how simple and clear is its explanation. To those who showed surprise that the history of Rome could become fashionable in Paris salons, I have always replied: My history has had its fortune because it was the history of Rome. Written with the same method and in the same style, a history of Venice, or Florence, or England, would not have had the same lot. One must not forget that the story of Rome occupies in the intellectual world a privileged place. Not only is it studied in all the schools of the civilised world; not only do nearly all states spend money to bring to light all the documentary evidence that the earth still conceals; but while all other histories are studied

128

fitfully, that of Rome is, so to speak, remade every fifty years, and whoever arrives at the right time to do the making can gain a reputation broader than that given to most historians.

There is, so to speak, in the history of Rome an eternal youth, and for the mind in what is commonly called European-American civilisation, it holds a peculiar attraction. From what deep sources springs this perennial youth? In what consists this particular force of attraction and renewal? It seems to me that the chief reason for the eternal fascination of the history of Rome is this, that it includes, as in a miniature drawn with simple lines, well defined, all the essential phenomena of social life; so that every age is able there to find its own image, its gravest problems, its intensest passions, its most pressing interests, its keenest struggles; therefore Roman history is forever modern, because every new age has only to choose that part which most resembles it, to find its own self.

In the intellectual history of the nineteenth century this leading phenomenon of our culture is clearly evident. If any one asked me why, during the past century, Roman history has proved so interesting, I should not hesitate to reply, "Because Europeans and Americans find there more than elsewhere what has been the greatest political upheaval of the hundred years that followed the French Revolution—the struggle between monarchy and republic." From the fervid admiration for the Roman Republic which animated the men of the French Revolution to the unmeasured Cæsarian apologies of Duruy and of Mommsen, from the ardent cult of Brutus to the detailed studies on the Roman administration of the first two centuries, all historians have studied and regarded Roman history mainly from the point of view of the struggle between the two principles that yet to-day rend in incurable discord the mind of old Europe and from which you have emerged fortunate! You are free, in a new world; you have ended the combat between the Latin principle of the impersonal state and the Oriental principle of the dynastic state; between the state conceived as the thing of all, belonging to every one and therefore of no one, and the state personified in a family of an origin higher and nobler than the common in which all authority derives from some hero-founder by a mysterious virtue unaccountable to reason and human philosophy; you have done with the conflict between the human state, simple, without pomp, without dramatic symbols—the republic as we men of the twentieth century understand it, and as you Americans conceive and practise it—and the monarchy of divine right, vainglorious, full of ceremonies and etiquette, despotic in internal constitution, which still exists in Europe under more or less spurious forms. Now it is easy to explain how, in an age in which the contest between these two conceptions and these two forms of the State was so warm, the history of Rome should so stir the mind.

In no other history do these two political forms meet each other in a more irreconcilable opposition of characters in extreme. The Republic, as Rome had founded it, was so impersonal that, in contrast with modern more democratic republics, it had not even a fixed bureaucracy, and all the public functions were exercised by elective magistrates—even the executive—from public works to the police-system. In the ancient monarchy which the Orient had created, the dynastic principle was so strong that the State was considered by inherent right the personal property of the sovereign, who might expand it, contract it, divide it among his sons and relatives, bequeathing his kingdom and his subjects as a land-owner disposes of his estate and his cattle. Furthermore, although to-day the sovereigns of Europe are pleased to treat quite familiarly with the good Lord, the rulers in the Orient were held to be gods in their own right.

Whence it is easy to understand how terrible must have been the struggle between the two principles so antagonistic, from the time when in the Empire, immeasurable and complicated, the institutions of the Republic proved inadequate to govern so many diverse peoples and territories so vast. The Romans kept on, as at first, rebelling at the idea of placing a man-god at the head of the State, themselves to become, when finally masters of the world, the slaves of a dynasty. The conflict between the two principles lasted a century, from Cæsar to Nero, filled the story of Rome with hideous tragedies, but ended with the truce of a glorious compromise; for Rome succeeded in putting into the monarchic constitution of empire some essentially republican ideas, among others, the idea of the indivisibility of the State. Not only Augustus and his family, but also the Flavians and the Antonines, never thought that the Empire belonged to them, that they might dispose of it like private property; on the contrary, they regarded it as an eternal and indivisible holding of the Roman people which they, as representatives of the *populus,* were charged to administer.

It is therefore easy, as I have said, to explain how, as never before, the history of Rome was looked upon as a great war between the monarchy and the republic. Indeed, the problem of the republic and the monarchy, always present to the minds of writers of the nineteenth century, has been perhaps the chief reason for the gravest mistakes committed by Roman historiography during this period—mistakes I have sought to correct. For example, the republicans have pinned their faith to all the absurd tales told by Suetonius and Tacitus about the family of the Cæsars, through preconceived hate for the monarchy; and the monarchists have exaggerated out of measure the felicity of the first two centuries of the Empire, to prove that the provinces lived happy under the monarchic administration as never before or after. Mommsen has fashioned an impossible Cæsar, almost making of that great demagogue a literary anticipation of Bismarck.

Little by little, however, as the contest between republic and monarchy gradually spent itself in Europe, in the last twenty-five years of the nineteenth century, the interest for histories of Rome conceived and written in this spirit, declined. The real reason why Mommsen and Duruy are to-day so little read, why at the beginning of the twentieth century Roman history no longer stirs enthusiasm through their books is, above all, this: that readers no longer find in those pages what corresponds directly to living reality. Therefore it was to be believed that Roman history had grown old and out of date; whereas, merely one of its perishing and deciduous forms had grown old, not the soul of it, which is eternally living and young. So true is this, that a writer had only to consider the old story from new points of view, for Cæsar and Antony, Lucullus and Pompey, Augustus and the laws of the year 18 B.C., to become subjects of fashionable conversation in Parisian drawing-rooms, in the most refined intellectual centre of the world.

It has never been difficult for me to realise that contemporary Europe and America, the Europe and America of railroads, industries, monstrous swift-growing cities, might find present in ancient Rome a part of their own very souls, restless, turbulent, greedy. In the Rome of the days of Cæsar, huge, agitated, seething with freedmen, slaves, artisans come from everywhere, crowded with enormous tenement-houses, run through from morning till night by a mad throng, eager for amusements and distractions; in that Rome where there jostled together an unnumbered population, uprooted from land, from family, from native country, and where from the press of so many men there fermented all the propelling energies of history and all the forces that destroy morality and life —vice and intellectuality, the imperialistic policy, deadly epidemics; in that changeable Rome, here splendid, there squalid; now magnanimous, and now brutal; full of grandeurs, replete with horrors; in that great city all the huge modern metropolises are easily refound, Paris and New York, Buenos Ayres and London, Melbourne and Berlin. Rome created the word that denotes this marvellous and monstrous phenomenon of history, the enormous city, the deceitful source of life and death — *urbs* — *the city*. Whence it is not strange that the countless *urbes* which the grand economic progress of the nineteenth century has caused to rise in every part of Europe and America look to Rome as their eldest sister and their dean.

Furthermore, into the history of Rome, the historic aristocracy of Europe may look as into the mirror of their own destiny, as everywhere they try to retain wealth and power, playing in the stock-exchange, marrying the daughters of millionaire brewers, giving themselves to commerce; a nobility that resorts, in the effort to preserve its prestige over the middle classes, to the expedients of the most reckless demagogy. Sulla, Lucullus, Pompey, Crassus, Antony, Cæsar, exemplify in stupendous types the aristocracy that seeks to conserve riches and power by audaciously employing the forces that menace its own destruction.

Several critics of my work, particularly the French, have observed that the policy of expansion made by Rome in the times of Cæsar, as I have described it, resembles closely the craze for imperialism that about ten years ago agitated England. It is true, for imperialism in the time of Cæsar was what has existed for the last half century in England—a means of which one part of the historic aristocracy availed itself to keep power and renew decaying prestige, satisfying material interests and flattering with intoxications of vanity the pride of the masses. So, too, the contesting parties in France—the socialist, which represents the labouring classes; the radical, which represents the middle classes; the progressive and the monarchic, which represent the wealthy burghers and the aristocracy—may discover some of their passions, their doings, their invectives, in the political warfare that troubled the age of Cæsar; in those scandals, those judicial trials, in that furor of pamphlets and discourses. This is so true, that in consequence my book met a singular fate in France; that of being adopted by each party as an argument in its own favour. Drumont made use of it to demonstrate to France what befalls a country when it allows its national spirit to be corrupted by foreign influx, seeking to persuade his fellow-citizens that the Jews in France do the same work of intellectual and moral dissolution that the Orientals brought about in Rome. Radical writers, like André Maurel, have sought arguments in my work to combat the colonial and imperialistic policy. The imperialists also, like Pinon, have looked for arguments to support their stand-point. Was I not merely demonstrating that the policy of expansion is a kind of universal and constant law, which periodically actualises itself through the working of the same forces, in the same ways?

It is not to be thought that the age of Cæsar, so disturbed, so stormy, is our only mirror in the story of Rome. When I write the account of the imperial society of the first and second centuries, our own time will be able to recognise even more of itself, to see what must be the future of Europe and America, if for a century or two they have no profound political and social upheavals. In that great *pax Romana* lasting two centuries, we may study with special facility a phenomenon to be found in all rich civilisations cultured and relatively at peace—the phenomenon to me the most important in contemporary European life, the feminising of all social life; that is, the victory of the feminine over the masculine spirit. Do not fancy that the feminists, the problems and the disputes they excite in modern society, are something quite new and peculiar to us; these are only special forms of a phenomenon more general, the growing influence that woman exercises on society, as civilisation, culture, and wealth steadily increase. Here, too, the history of Rome is luminously clear. In it we see evolving that vast contest between the feminine spirit and the masculine, which is one of the essential phenomena in all human history. We see the masculine spirit—the spirit of domination, of force, of mastery, of daring—ruling complete, when the small community had to fight its first hard battles against nature and men. The father commanded then as monarch in his family; the woman was without right, liberty, personality; had but to obey, to bear children and rear them. But success, power, wealth, greater security, imperceptibly loosened the narrow bondage of the first struggles; then the feminine spirit—the spirit of freedom, of pleasure, of art, of revolt against tradition—gradually acquired strength, and began bit by bit to undermine at its bases the stern masculine rule.

The hard conflict of two centuries is sown with tragedies and catastrophes. Supported by tradition, exasperated by the ever bolder revolts of woman, the masculine spirit every now and then went mad; and brutally tore away her costly jewels and tried to deny her soft raiment and rare perfumes; and when she had already grown accustomed to appearing in the world and shining there, he willed to drive her back into the house, and put beside her there on guard the fieriest threats of law. Sometimes, despairing, he filled Rome with his laments; protested that the liberty of the woman cost the man too dear; cried out that the bills of the dressmaker and the jeweller would send Rome, the Empire, the world, to ruin. In vain, with wealth, in a civilisation full of Oriental influences, woman grew strong, rose, and invaded all society, until in the vast Empire of the first and second centuries, at the climax of her power, with beauty, love, luxury, culture, prodigality, and mysticism she dominated and dissolved a society which in the refinements of wealth and intellectuality had lost the sharp virtues of the pioneer.

It is unnecessary to dilate further on this point; it will be better rather to dwell a moment on the causes and the effects of this singular phenomenon. The history of Rome has been and can be so rich, so manifold, so universal, because in its long record ancient Rome gathered up into itself, welded, fused, the most diverse elements of social life, from all peoples and all regions with which it came into contact. It knew continued war and interrupted peace for centuries. It held united under its vast sway, states decrepit with the oldest of civilisations, and peoples hardly out of primitive barbarism. It exploited with avidity the intelligence, the laboriousness, the science of the former; the physical force, the war-valour and the daring of the latter; it absorbed the vices, the habits, the ideas of the Hellenised Orient, and transfused them in the untamed Occident. Taking men, ideas, money, everywhere and from every people, it created first an empire, then a literature, an architecture, an administration, and a new religion, that were the most tremendous synthesis of the ancient world. So the Roman world turned out vaster and more complex than the Greek, although never assuming proportions exceeding the power of the human mind; and as it grew, it kept that precious quality, wanting in the Greek, unity; hence, the lucid clearness of Roman history. There is everything in it, and everything radiates from one centre, so that comprehension is easy.

Without doubt it would be rash to declare that the history of Rome alone may serve as the outline of universal history. It is quite likely that there may be found another history that possesses the same two qualities for which that of Rome is so notable — universality and unity — but one thing we may affirm: up to this time the history of Rome alone has fulfilled this office of universal compendium, which explains how it has always been studied by the learned and lettered of every part of the civilised European-American world, and how in modern intellectual life it is the history universal and cosmopolitan *par excellence.* This condition of things has a much greater practical importance than is supposed. Indeed it would be a serious mistake to believe that cosmopolitan catholicity is an ideal dower purely of Roman history, for which all the sons of Rome may congratulate themselves as of a thing doing honour only to their stirp. This universality forms part, I should say, of the material patrimony of all the Latin stock; we may number it in the historic inventory of all the good things the sons of Rome possess and of all their reasonable hopes for the future.

This affirmation may at first appear to you paradoxical, strange, and obscure, but I think a short exposition will suffice to clear it. The universality of the history of Rome, the ease of finding in it models in miniature of all our life, will have this effect, that classical studies remain the educational foundation of the intelligent classes in all European-American civilisation. These studies may be reformed; they may be, as they ought, restricted to a smaller number of persons; but if it is not desired — as of course it cannot be — that in the future all men be purely technical capacities and merely living machines to create material riches; if, on the contrary, it is desired that in every nation the chosen few that govern have a philosophical consciousness of universal life, no means is better suited to instil this philosophic consciousness than the study of ancient Rome, its history, its civilisation, its laws, its politics, its art, and its religions, exactly because Rome is the completest and most lucid synthesis of universal life.

Classical studies are one of the most powerful means of intellectual and moral influence on the Anglo-Saxon and German civilisations that the Latins possess, representing under modern conditions, for the Latin nations, a kind of intellectual entail inherited from their ancestors. The young Germans and Englishmen who study Greek and Latin, who translate Cicero or construe Horace, assimilate the Latin spirit, are brought ideally and morally nearer to us, are prepared without knowing it to receive our intellectual and social influence in other fields, are made in greater or less degree to resemble us. Indeed, it can be said, that, material interests apart, Rome is still in the mental field the strongest bond that holds together the most diverse peoples of Europe; that it unites the French, the English, the Germans, in an ideal identity which overcomes in part the diversity in speech, in traditions, in geographical situation, and in history. If common classical studies did not make kindred spirits of the upper classes in England, France, and Germany, the Rhine and the Channel would divide three nations mentally so different as to be impenetrable each to another.

Therefore the cosmopolitan universality of Roman history is a kind of common good which the Latin races ought to defend with all their might, having care that no other history usurp its place in contemporary culture; that it remain the typical outline, the ideal model of universal history in the education of coming generations. The Latin civilised world has need that every now and then an historian arise to reanimate the history of Rome, in order to maintain its continued supremacy in the education of the intelligent; to prevent other histories from usurping this pre-eminence.

It is useless to cherish illusions as to the task: its accomplishment has become much more arduous than it was fifty years ago; perhaps because the masses have acquired greater power in every part of the European-American world, and democracy advances more or less rapidly, invading everything—the democracy of the technical man, the merchant, the workman, the well-to-do burgher, all of whom easily hold themselves aloof from a culture in itself aristocratic. The accomplishment will become always more and more arduous; for Roman studies, feeling the new generations becoming estranged from them, have for the last twenty-five years tended to take refuge in the tranquil cloisters of learning, of archæology, in the discreet concourse of a few wise men, who voluntarily flee the noises of the world, Fatal thought! Ancient Rome ought to live daily in the mind of the new social classes that lead onward; ought to irradiate its immortal light on the new worlds that arise from the deeps of the modern age, on pain of undergoing a new destruction more calamitous than that caused by the hordes of Alaric. The day when the history of Rome and its monuments may be but material for erudition to put into the museums by the side of the bricks of the palace of Khorsabad, the cuneiform inscriptions, and the statues of the kings of Assyria, Latin civilisation will be overwhelmed by a fatal catastrophe.

To hinder the extinction of the great light of Rome in the world, to prolong indefinitely this ideal survival, which is the continuation of its material Empire, destroyed centuries ago, there is but one way—to renew historic studies of Rome, and to maintain intact their universal value which forms part of common culture. This is what I have tried to do, seeking to lead back to Roman history the many minds estranged from it, distracted by so many cares and anxieties and present questionings, and to fulfil a solemn duty to my fatherland and the grand traditions of Latin culture. If other histories can grow old, it is indeed the more needful, exactly because it serves to educate new generations, to reanimate Roman history, incorporating in it the new facts constantly discovered by archæological effort, infusing it with a larger and stronger philosophical spirit, carrying into it the matured experience of the world, which learns not only by studying but also by living.

I do not hesitate to say that every half-century there opens among civilised peoples a contest to find the new conception of Roman history, which, suited to the changed needs, may revivify classical studies; a competition followed by no despicable prize, the intellectual influence that a people may exercise on other peoples by means of these studies. To win in this contest we must never forget, as too many of us have done in the past thirty years, that a man can rule and refashion the world from the depths of a library, but only on condition that he does not immure himself there; that, while the physical sciences propose to understand matter in order to transform it, historico-philosophical discipline has for its end action upon the mind and the will; that philosophical ideas and historic teachings are but seeds shut up to themselves unless they enter the soil of the universal intellectual life.

No: the time-stained marbles of Rome must not end beside cuneiform-inscribed bricks or Egyptian mummies, in the vast dead sections of archæological halls; they must serve to pave for our feet the way that leads to the future. Therefore nothing could have been pleasanter or more grateful to me, after receiving the invitation tendered me by the *Collège de France,* and that from South America, than to accept the invitation of the First Citizen of the United States to visit this world which is being formed.

In Paris, that wonderful metropolis of the Latin world, I had the joy, the highest reward for my long, hard labour, to show to the incredulous how much alive the supposedly dead history of Rome still is, when on those unforgettable days so cosmopolite a public gathered from every part of the city in the small plain hall of the old and august edifice. Coming into your midst, I feel that the history of Rome lives not only in the interest with which you have followed these lectures, but also, even if in part without clear cognisance, in things here, in the life you lead, in what you accomplish. The heritage of Rome is, for the peoples of America still more than for those of Europe, an heredity not purely artistic and literary, but political and social, which exercises the most beneficent influence on your history. In a certain sense it might be said that America is to-day politically, more than Europe, the true heir of Rome; that the new world is nearer — by apparent paradox — to ancient Rome than is Europe. Among the most important facts, however little noticed, in the history of the nineteenth century, I should number this: that the Republic, the human state considered as the common property of all—the great political creation of ancient Rome—is reborn here in America, after having died out in Europe. The Latin seed, lying buried for so many centuries beneath the ruins of the ancient world, like the grains of wheat buried in Egyptian tombs, transported from the other side of the ocean, has sprung up in the land that Columbus discovered. If there had been no Rome; if Rome had wholly perished in the great barbarian catastrophe; if in the Renaissance there had not been found among the ruins of the ancient world, together with beautiful Greek statues and manuscripts, this great political idea, there would to-day be no Republic in North America. With the word would probably have perished also the idea and the thing; and there is no assurance that men would have been able so easily and so well to rediscover it by their own effort.

I am a student and not a flatterer. I therefore confess to you frankly, ending these lectures, that I do not belong to that number of Europeans who most enthusiastically admire things American. I think that Americans in general, in North America as in South, so readily recognise in themselves a sufficient number of virtues, that we Europeans hardly need help them in the belief, easy and agreeable to all, that they stand first in the world. Having come from an old society, which has a long historical experience, the most vivid impression made upon me in the two Americas has been just that of entering into a society provided with but meagre historical experience, which therefore easily deludes itself, mistaking for signs of heroic energy and proofs of a finished superiority, the passing advantages of an order chiefly economic, which come from the singular economic condition of the world. In a word, I do not believe that you are superior to Europe in as many things as you think; but a superiority I do recognise, great and, for me at least, indisputable, in the political institutions with which you govern yourselves. The Republic, which you have made to live again, here in this new land, is the true political form worthy of a civilised people, because the only one that is rational and plastic; while the monarchy, the form of government yet ruling so many parts of

Europe, is a mixture of mysticism and barbarity, which European interests seek in vain to justify with sophistries unworthy the high grade of culture to which the Continent has attained. To search out the reasons why the old Oriental monarchy holds on so tenaciously in Europe, still threatening the future, would be useless here; certain it is that, when you meet any European other than a Frenchman or a Swiss, you can feel yourselves as superior to him in political institutions as the Roman *civis* in the times of the Republic felt himself above the Asiatic slave of absolute monarchy. This superiority—never forget it!—you owe to Rome; for its possession, be grateful to the city that has encircled you with such glory, by infusing so tenacious a life into the

"Respublica."

ENDNOTES

"CORRUPTION" IN ANCIENT ROME
AND ITS COUNTERPART
IN MODERN HISTORY

[1] The Greatness and Decline of Rome. 5 vols. New York and London.

INDEX

SUGGESTED READING

BOATWRIGHT, M. T., R. J. A. TALBERT, AND D. J. GARGOLA. *The Romans: From Village to Empire.* New York: Oxford University Press, 2004.

FERREO, GUGLIELMO. *Militarism.* London: Ward Lock, 1902.

---. *The Life of Caesar.* Trans. A. E. Zimmern. London: Allen & Unwin, 1933.

---. *The Principles of Power.* Trans. Theodore R. Jaeckel. New York: G. P. Putnam's Sons, 1942.

---. *The Reconstruction of Europe.* Trans. Theodore R. Jaeckel. New York: G. P. Putnam's Sons, 1941.

---. *The Unity of the World.* Trans. Howard Coxe. London: Jonathan Cape, 1931.

GIBBON, EDWARD. *Decline and Fall of the Roman Empire.* Ed. G. B. Piranesi. New York: Random House, 2003.

GOLDSWORTHY, ADRIAN. *In the Name of Rome.* London: Phoenix Press, 2004.

---. The Complete Roman Army. New York: Thames & Hudson, 2003.

GRANT, MICHAEL. *Sick Caesars.* New York: Barnes & Noble Books, 2003.

---. *The Roman Emperors.* New York: Barnes & Noble Books, 1997.

LIVY. *Early History of Rome.* Trans. Aubrey De Selincourt. New York: Penguin, 2002.

MOMMSEN, THEODOR. *The History of Rome.* Trans. W. P. Dickinson. London: Routledge, 1996.

PARENTI, MICHAEL. *The Assassination of Julius Caesar.* New York: New Press, 2003.

PLUTARCH. *Makers of Rome*. Trans. Ian Scott-Kilvert. New York: Penguin, 1978.

---. *The Fall of the Roman Republic*. Trans. Rex Warner. New York: Penguin, 1972.

POLYBIUS. *The Rise of the Roman Empire*. Trans. Ian Scott-Kilvert. New York: Penguin, 1980.

SAID, EDWARD. *Orientalism*. London: Routledge & Kegan Paul, 1978.

SUETONIUS. *The Lives of the Caesars*. Trans. J. C. Rolfe. New York: Barnes & Noble Books, 2004.

TACITUS. *Histories*. Trans. Kenneth Wellesley. New York: Penguin, 1976.

---. *The Annals of Imperial Rome*. Trans. Michael Grant. New York: Penguin, 1976.

VEBLEN, THORSTEIN. *The Theory of the Leisure Class*. London: Routledge, 1994.

WEBER, MAX. *The Protestant Ethic and the Spirit of Capitalism*. Trans. Talcott Parsons. London: Routledge, 2001.